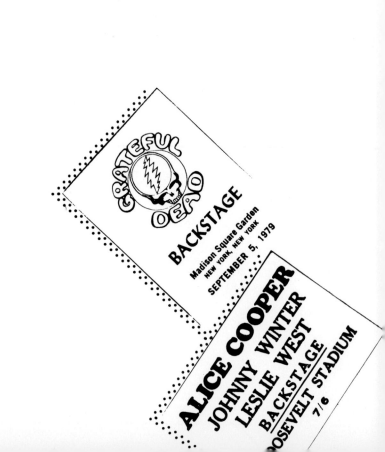

POURIN' IT ALL OUT

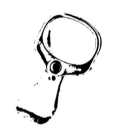

POURIN' IT ALL OUT

JAY SAPORITA

Riverside Community College
Library
4800 Magnolia Avenue
Riverside, CA 92506

CITADEL PRESS   Secaucus, New Jersey

First edition
Copyright © 1980 by Jay Saporita
All rights reserved

Published by Citadel Press
A division of Lyle Stuart Inc.
120 Enterprise Ave., Secaucus, N.J. 07094

In Canada: General Publishing Co. Limited
Don Mills, Ontario

Manufactured in the United States of America by
Halliday Lithograph, West Hanover, Mass.

Designed by Peter Davis

Copy edited by Paul Busby

Library of Congress Cataloging in Publication Data
Saporita, Jay.
    Pourn' it all out.
    1. Rock music—History and criticism. I. Title.
ML3534.S26   784.5'4   80-12643
ISBN 0-8065-0696-2
ISBN 0-8065-0729-2 (pbk.)

To my family,
especially Pam,

And to Linda:
You take my breath away

CONTENTS

Introduction	13
Billy Joel	17
Easy (Eddie) Money	31
Meat Loaf	43
Van Morrison	51
Jackson Browne	55
Feed Your Head	59
Punk	65
The Proper Lament for the Premier Punk	79
Backstage Wave	83
Elvis Costello	89
Steely Dan	101
Bruce Springsteen	103
Springsteen Live!	125
The Road Way	141
Radio, Radio	145
George Benson	153
Stevie Wonder	161
Feed Your Body	169
The Grateful Dead	181
Elvis, Alone, in Memphis	191
Loose Lips	195
Trade Talk: A Glossary	201

ACKNOWLEDGMENTS

Many thanks to the following people, who have always been more than generous with their time: Larry Solters, Charlie Frick, Joe Dera, Vin Scelsa, T. Allen, R. Deans, T. Cowan, Parker Kates, Howard and Helen Lemke, and the Queen Hotel; and to Graham Parker, whose talent led to the title of this book.

Thank you to everyone at Monarch Entertainment, especially John Scher, Mary Glogoza, and Cy Kocis.

Thank you to all those at *High Times* magazine and *The Aquarian Weekly* for their generosity and cooperation.

. . . Performers are just children
with a bad sense of direction
they stumble into the spotlight
searchin' for affection
Now fame has got your number
lonesome's stole your name
And you're wonderin' when you'll fumble
and blow the whole ball game

    "The Price That Princes Pay"
                Rich Deans

Rock's most coveted possession: the backstage pass. It allows an
"outsider" unimpeded movement within the shrouded behind-the-
scenes world where idols dwell.

(Photo: K Stechow)

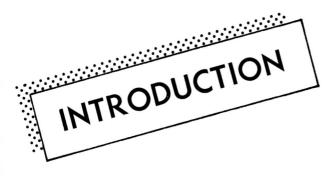

INTRODUCTION

Rock 'n' roll is perhaps the most intensely personal art experience in contemporary society. Fans' loyalties are fierce; they attach as much significance to their idols' beliefs and perceptions (as presented through their music) as a more traditional person might to the preachings of a spiritual leader. In many ways John Lennon was correct when, years ago, he quipped that the Beatles were "bigger than Christ." What Lennon meant, of course (he was internationally misunderstood), was not that the Beatles *warranted* more popularity than Christ, but that the masses had *accorded* them more.

If anything, the power of rock has increased tenfold since Lennon's statement. It is estimated that in the United States alone more than fifty million persons take rock 'n' roll very seriously; that is, it is their primary arts-related interest. Despite industry worries of impending inflation, the finances are still awesome: In 1979 the record industry reported revenues just above the four-billion-dollar mark. CBS (Columbia Records) alone took in a billion dollars. Warner Bros./ Elektra-Atlantic (WEA), Arista, and Asylum Records are reportedly doing well, although not quite so well as the mighty CBS.

The herculean finances do not stop at the industry level. Paul McCartney's newest contract brought him ten million dollars. Stevie Wonder was acquired by Motown for twelve million dollars. Both were outdone by Paul Simon; he left Columbia Records for Warner Bros. with a vault-filling thirteen million dollars.

Today's rock personalities inhabit a world not unlike the world of major corporation heads. A group of highly skilled, highly paid lawyers, accountants, managers, and producers, usually brought together under a single roof as a "production company," are maintained in order to ensure that these huge sums of money constantly increase.

All rock's top stars hold the distinction of being heavy investors in real estate, restaurants, oil fields, and other areas. But the business

end of rock 'n' roll means little to the fan. To him and her,
the music is the entire message. Further, for the most part the nearest
any of these aficionados has come to his or her hero is a first-row
seat at a concert. Personal contact between fans and performers
is rare. Accordingly, fans have surrounded their heroes with legends,
using their songs and the material available in press interviews
as the basis on which they came to construct their heroes'
personalities.

There are times when the legend and the celebrity match. There
are just as many times when they don't.

What follows are interviews, profiles, anecdotes, and vignettes,
all concerned with a single theme—the world of rock 'n' roll.
Its heroes are here; some spoke at length about their careers and
their lifestyles, some spoke briefly but with sharp insight concerning
their profession, and some preferred to be interviewed and
watched "in action," as it were. All emerged as very real *human
beings* whether or not their true characters match their legends.

This book, though factual in content, is meant to be read as one
would read a novel—from cover to cover. In that way, the reader
will come to understand that rock 'n' roll consists of the careful
combination of two ingredients—fact and fantasy. It could not exist
without either of them.

Billy Joel

BILLY JOEL

AN ANGRY YOUNG MAN

The tale has all the earmarks of an overzealous press agent's fabrication—a deluge of pathos that makes for good copy. As a matter of fact, if it weren't for the irrefutable facts behind the tale, it would be dismissed as no more than a harmless scam, an unsuccessful attempt to inject even more color into a now over-whelmingly famous human being.

But the anecdote's veracity is made all the more undeniable considering that a close friend of mine played a small, albeit unintentional, part in the matter.

In 1972, an unexpected change in jobs forced my friend to move to Los Angeles. To hear him tell it, the moment his jet skimmed into the black scum of smog on its approach to the Los Angeles airport, he knew he had made a mistake. Bumper-to-bumper-to-bumper freeway traffic didn't do much to allay his apprehensions.

Almost from his first day on the West Coast, he took to drinking; it wasn't the boozy-Bowery plunge, but the liquid-lunch-followed-by-an-evening-in-the-cocktail-lounge escape route. One evening he called me from his favorite nightspot, a place called the Executive Room. In a slurred, excited voice he asked me if I'd ever heard of a piano player—singer named Bill Martin. "I know I've seen him somewhere before," he shouted.

I assured him that I knew of no one in the business with that name. I further insisted that if I did know a performer, he certainly wouldn't be playing cocktail music in a piano bar in Los Angeles. Convinced, my friend hung up, mumbling, "I asked him if he was from New York or something, but he wouldn't say."

Five years passed. My friend, not too much the worse for his Los Angeles experience, had returned to Manhattan. We were backstage at a benefit concert, feasting on a huge repast and marveling at the plethora of celebrities present. Suddenly a puffy-eyed, slightly paunchy character drifted past us. He had a beer in his

hand. He was wearing jeans, sneakers, a dress shirt, and a
New York Yankees baseball cap.

"*Who's that!*" my friend yelped.

"Billy Joel," I answered.

"That's him!" he yelled.

"That's who?"

"The guy I told you about. The piano player in Los Angeles. That's
Bill Martin."

"That *was* me," Joel allows, not so much ashamed of the circum-
stance as he is angry that it ever had to exist. "I don't remember
your friend . . . but I was probably in worse shape than him
anyway. I don't really remember too much about the whole episode.
. . . I was kinda in an alcoholic daze the whole time I was there."

Having recently returned from a record-breaking European tour,
Joel spends most afternoons in the Manhattan office of his production
company, Home Run Systems.

His 1977 album *The Stranger* has reached sales of more than four
million, and a single from the album ("Just the Way You Are") was
awarded a 1978 Grammy for Best Song. The follow-up LP,
52nd Street, shipped gold and has been certified double platinum.
He is an extremely popular young man, just thirty years old, who,
through hook and crook, *finally* has a firm hold on his career
and its future.

But matters weren't always so bright, and therein lies the story
behind his escape to Los Angeles. In 1971, after years of dues
paying (with a group called *The Hassles* and one strange album

18

entitled *Attila*), Joel made a decision to pursue a solo career. "I got hooked up with Artie Ripp and Family Productions," Joel explains, rubbing his temples with his hand. A long, low sigh indicates that he's told this story one too many times. "I can't even begin to tell you the troubles I had. First, I was twenty-one, okay? Old enough to sign my life away *legally* but still young enough to be an asshole. Anyway, we went out to Record Plant West and made the album, and then, when I listened to the master tapes, I realized that my voice was about three octaves higher than it's humanly possible for me to sing! I got a hold of Artie, told him something's wrong with my voice. I don't *sound* like that. Artie said, 'It's okay. It sounds all right; don't worry about it.' So they went ahead and released the thing."

The album was called *Cold Spring Harbor*; perhaps *Cold Spring Horror* would have been more apt. Joel was correct in his assumption that the finished product contained a grievous error. Ripp admits that during the final production work he found that one of the recording machines was running too slow, another too fast. When he set about mixing the master tape, all the songs came out with an accelerated beat. Nonetheless, he chose to release the album. To add insult to injury, he sent Joel on the road with a pickup band, with promotional backing that was all but nonexistent.

Joel decided he'd had it with the recording industry. "I wasn't able to deal with the record business," he readily admits, " 'cause that's all that it is—a fuckin' *business*. Just like any other business. I didn't understand that, and I didn't particularly *want* to. I'm a musician, not a businessman." So he fled.

"I didn't want to make a big deal out of it, but I couldn't handle what was going on, so I split to the West Coast [he had been living in Oyster Bay, Long Island] and got a gig playing as Bill Martin. I just didn't care any more. I was very disillusioned by then."

Joel stayed at the Executive Room for a little more than half a year. Eventually Family Productions (which hadn't been able to *find*

19

The good life.

Joel during that time) was persuaded to relinquish his contract,
but not before a compromise was reached wherein the production
company would continue to receive royalties on all future
Billy Joel records.

Joel returned to New York and signed with Columbia. In November
1973, he released *Piano Man*. The album's title single garnered
immediate attention, the result of which was a year of almost
constant air play. Yet sales were, at the best, decent. "People always
figured that 'Piano Man' made me rich or somethin'," Joel jokes.
"There's always been a big myth about the *sales* of that record.
I mean, *everybody* played it—I was very grateful for that—but
the record never got beyond the Top Twenty on any of the charts."

Streetlife Serenade followed *Piano Man*. As with its predecessor,
Streetlife contained a single ("The Entertainer") that received wide
air play, but again sales did not reflect the media's attention.
Familiar fears began to set in: "I didn't seem to be able to get
through. I couldn't get an identity going—people thought I was
Harry Chapin or something. What no one seemed to realize was that
I was also writing hard-rock stuff, some controversial things . . .
but there were a lot of people who were just writing me off.
Michael Stewart [the producer of *Piano Man* and *Streetlife Serenade*]
didn't give me much help; neither did the company.

"It was the business trip all over again. Ya know, if you have a hit
record, great, they love you. If you don't, it's like, 'Well, come on,
let's come up with a hit.' Everything is *hit*, ya gotta have a *hit*.
I couldn't seem to get anybody to listen to what I wanted, what I
thought would help my career. I needed to get out on the road
with a band and *play!* But they kept on thinking, 'Billy Joel,
sensitive songwriter. We gotta get that on record. That's the image.'
It was bullshit all over again."

It began to look as if Joel was destined to spend his professional

22

life on the periphery of success. He moved to upstate New York
with his wife, Elizabeth, to work on his fourth LP, *Turnstiles.* Joel's
streak of bad luck continued. He wanted veteran producer
Phil Ramone to take the reins on *Turnstiles,* but Ramone was
committed to another project.

Joel joined forces with Caribou Studios' J. W. Guercio (Chicago's
producer) but soon found that he and Guercio didn't see eye to eye.
"He was like a part of the Hollywood factory, and I couldn't get
it going. I don't know, maybe it was me. I got along pretty well
with him, but I just didn't feel anything was happenin'."

Guercio and Joel split in the midst of *Turnstiles.* Joel took over the
remainder of the production work himself. He produced perhaps the
first recording that sounded like *Billy Joel.* He also found
Richie Cannata, Doug Stegmeyer, and Liberty DeVitto—three
musicians with whom he felt comfortable enough to propose an
ongoing band.

Yet for all the critical notices *Turnstiles* was accorded, its sales
did not exceed a couple of hundred thousand. It was the fall of 1976,
and in Joel's words, "Things were a complete mess." As happened
in the case of Springsteen and his problems with Laurel Canyon
Productions, in the early part of his career Joel had signed away
ownership rights of his own songs. His financial situation was
certainly not stable. He hadn't yet reached the point where he
could maintain his proposed band.

Joel was exasperated. In a moment of irritation he blurted to his wife,
"Why don't you manage me? You've been around long enough.
I must be doing something wrong; maybe you can figure it out."

It was a plea made in jest, Joel recalls, but within a week
Elizabeth had established herself as Billy Joel's personal manager,
calling the company Home Run—a reference to its inception in their

92nd Street apartment. Elizabeth set about to wipe the slate clean. It took almost three years, but Billy Joel has emerged at the helm of his own career and finances. Elizabeth realized that her husband was in desperate need of a recording situation in which he could be free to let loose. She acquired the services of Phil Ramone, a producer with whom Billy felt utterly at ease. "Phil understood what I was going for immediately," Joel beams. "His presence in the studio brought the best out in me."

Ramone and Joel created a precocious offspring, *The Stranger*, released in September 1977. Within three months, Billy Joel became one of the biggest-selling, best-known male songwriters in America. He had arrived.

A DETERMINED ADULT:

I don't need you to worry for me 'cause I'm alright
I don't want you to tell me it's time to come home
I don't care what you say anymore 'cause I'm alright
Go ahead with your own life and leave me alone
  "My Life"
  Billy Joel

With the solid success of *The Stranger* and *52nd Street* behind him, Joel resembles a contender after he's won the championship bout—he's cocky but not overbearing; he's opinionated and unabashedly pleased with his triumph.

He's still something of a prankster, a holdover from his youth. "I was never really a hood. My brother and his friends were the real hoods—they were *mean*. Me and my friends sorta followed our brothers around—you know, kinda imitating them. We didn't fight or nothing. We just fucked around. We sniffed glue, yeah. We all had phony proof so we could buy beer . . . but we was pretty harmless."

24

In addition to his early interest in playing baseball and in boxing, he started playing piano as a youngster. "I was fortunate. By the time I was fourteen I was making money as a musician. I knew then that I wasn't gonna live an ordinary life—no factory job or any of that. I knew I had the chops; I knew I played well. I didn't know whether or not I was gonna hit it big, but it didn't matter so long as I could make a living playin' music."

When he was fourteen, he saw James Brown perform at Harlem's Apollo Theatre. The image is a humorous one—a pudgy white kid immersed in a sea of blacks, eyes wide as Brown tore the place up. "It was a little hairy," he remembers, "but Brown blew me away. The footwork, the precision, the beat . . . and all that screaming."

Brown's all-out-assault style is reflected in Joel's own stage show. Watching Joel work is a study in aerobic-rock; he does not pause for a moment. The pace of his concerts is furious, incessant. "I love to play, I love an audience right *there*, feeding back at me. I'm not what you'd call a delicate piano player. I don't just play with my fingers—I put my whole body into it. I like to hear the thing scream. I know a lot of guys who break guitar strings— I break a lotta *piano* strings. I don't think there are too many guys doin' that!"

The length and effort involved in his performances are of paramount importance to him: "I've been around rock 'n' roll for a long time. I've been personally involved with playing for nine, ten years. I know most the rock stars, and I'll tell you, a lot of them have this contempt for their audiences. They think they're all a bunch of jerks. I don't buy that. I happen to think my people, the people who are into me, are intelligent. And they won't take any shit, so I don't give them any. I'll play until I collapse every fuckin' night if they want. I'll *come back* after that and start all over again! I *like* to play—I crave it. When we take intermissions, I get very upset. It's kinda like *coitus interruptus*—who the hell wants to stop when you're goin' at it?"

Joel in concert.

He approaches songwriting with the same intensity, becoming
infused within the muse. "Writing's not very easy for me. It's hard
for me to get to that space where the words start to flow. I don't
particularly *like* writing; it's very difficult. When I have to do it,
I go around kicking things, drinking, being obnoxious. . . . I sorta lose
myself. I don't shave. I get up in the morning, gulp down some
coffee, and sit at the piano. If I'm lucky somethin' will come.
If not, well, I gotta bitch around a little bit more until it starts to
happen. I'm not a lot of fun to be around when I'm writin'."

There are still remnants of the wise-ass, chip-on-the-shoulder kid
within Joel. For all of his love of music, his disdain for the music
industry remains constant. "Look," he explains, his eyes narrowing,
his features falling into a sneer, "there's a whole personality
machine out there. And it's all bullshit. They put you on the cover
of *Newsweek* or *Time* or *Rolling Stone,* and all of a sudden you're
great. It doesn't matter who you are or what you do—it just matters
that there you are for the whole world to see. You must be
somebody or you wouldn't've made the cover, right? It becomes a
parade of personalities. And that's bullshit. I'm not a personality;
I'm me. You want to know what I'm like—listen to my songs,
come hear me play. But forget all that personality crap."

As if taken aback by his own ferocity, Joel pauses, shakes his head
in dismay, and laughs aloud. His secretary indicates that he has
another appointment in a few minutes. He stretches, acknowledging
her message, and politely asks that the interview draw to a close.
"Sorry about that outburst," he says, rising. "It's just that . . .
I don't know, after a while it gets to you. You know, 'Billy Joel
thinks this,' 'Billy Joel thinks that,' and on and on. I get bored as shit
talking about Billy Joel for the forty thousandth time. I'd rather
get drunk."

Eddie Money

EASY (EDDIE) MONEY

It's becoming increasingly difficult to believe that the lanky, long-haired rowdy sitting next to me was once a New York City cop. Here we are, six of us, crammed into a barely alive Chevy, ripping along Manhattan's Fifth Avenue all but daring the traffic lights to trip us up, two joints overwhelming the car with smoke, and to make matters worse, we're greeting every woman we pass with a play-ground fertility cry, a piercing, obscene whoop.

But nothing can convince Eddie Money, the aforementioned rowdy, that there exists the very real possibility that all of us will be busted if we don't calm down a bit. Money's a transplanted New Yorker (he's spent the last half decade in northern California) and, like most city kids, knows that the authorities are much too concerned with "real crime" to even bother with us. "Besides," he shouts, elbowing me in the ribs, the fritz of a full can of Budweiser anointing the dashboard, "I still got my PBA card with me. The cops ain't gonna hassle us. Don't worry about it."

We are all more than a little inebriated; something Money's mentor, the mighty Bill Graham, rock's premier impresario, would most likely frown upon. Not that Graham need worry—two hours from now Money will play to a sold-out crowd at Madison Square Garden's Felt Forum, where more than five thousand fans (a good many of them screaming young women) will demand two encores.

Money's handsome, heavy-lidded, dark-eyed look, the same look that catapulted Presley into the hearts of millions, has captured the tender feminine hearts. His entire onstage manner is a throwback to the days of the crooners, updated to include the power and passion of rock. His music notwithstanding (certainly he can write good, solid, appealing tunes, as the sales of more than three million of his two LPs indicate), Money knows his audience. A result of more than a dozen years working every night in bar bands, he knows exactly what the audience wants. He's a tease, a hard yet cute guy whom every girl wants to take home and care for.

31

He once told me, "I grew up watching the Rascals, the Vagrants, and all that blue-eyed soul stuff, in the days when the front man, the lead singer, was emphasized. I like to flirt; I like the idea that I'm up there and all those girls are watchin' me. Hey, that's all right. I *like* girls!"

That's good, Eddie, but right now we're roaring uptown, heading to a spacious awaiting hotel suite for some preshow R and R, and I can't get rid of this creeping paranoia that we are going to be stopped by Manhattan's finest.

"This is excellent pot," a voice offers from the overstuffed back seat, adding anxiety to my paranoia. There's a murmur of agreement.

"Hey," Money intones, handing me another beer, "I told you not to worry—nothin's gonna happen. Besides, we're suppose to be doin' an interview, right?"

Right.

"Oh, yeah," he responds, "that cop thing's true, man. See, my dad was a cop, his father before him, his before that. It sorta runs in the family. It was kinda just *understood* that I'd become one. So I did. Well, actually, I *almost* did. I went to the academy, graduated, and got a job as a typist at the Thirteenth Precinct. That was cool. But, you know, I kept on gettin' hassled by the other guys, I guess 'cause my hair was longer than theirs. I wasn't always alert, if you know what I mean. I was playin' in a band at night, so I was always like half asleep. I was gettin' kinda tired of the job. I was thinkin' of splittin' anyway, and when that *thing* came up, I just took off for California."

"Thing?"

"Yeah, well, I used to use the typewriter to write letters to my friends, right? So one day I wrote my friend this big long letter about the great pot I'd been smokin', and somehow . . . I don't know, I must've left it around or somethin'. Anyway, somehow this sergeant found it, and . . . well, things didn't look too cool, so I took off to San Francisco!"

"In other words," I ask, noticing what appears to be an unmarked police car pulling up behind us, "they could probably still be wonderin' what ever happened to you."

"Hey, I never thought of that. But naw, don't worry. Like I said, my whole family's on the force!"

Somehow, we've settled into the hotel. The short journey from car through lobby to the suite is a forgotten blur. The only sound I can recall is the distinct crack of the seal of a bottle of Jack Daniel's being opened.

"I gotta take a shower," Money tells me. "Keep talkin'. I can hear ya."

I begin to shout questions through a hot, heavy mist. "Your first meeting with Bill Graham wasn't exactly a friendly one."

"Yeah, you heard about that, huh? Well, look, when I first got to California I was a radical. I lived on the outskirts of Berkeley— Berserkley, we called it—and, like, my parents had gone to the right, and I just went very far left. Every other day there was a rally for somebody or other. Free Me, Free You, Free *Anybody*—I didn't care. You know, I had this *attitude*. And I was playing music out there, so one day my friend and me tried to sneak into a show at Winterland, and we got caught by a couple of Bill's goons.

"The next thing I know they're handcuffing us, and here comes Graham! He looks pissed! So I just took off—cuffs and all. I didn't

33

Eddie Money

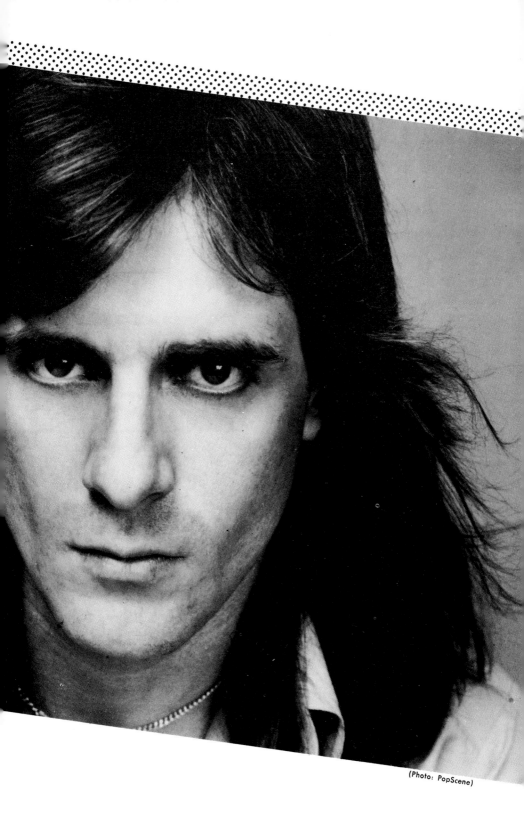

(Photo: PopScene)

want to get in bad with that sucker. I mean, as far as I was concerned, Bill Graham *was* rock 'n' roll in California. I figured if he caught me, I'd be through!''

"But you ended up being the first act signed to his production company."

"I know. That's crazy, huh? You see what happened was that Graham used to hold these amateur nights at Winterland. Sorta like open auditions. I played at one, and the next thing I knew I was in Bill's office bein' offered a contract. The whole time I'm standin' there thinkin' to myself, *Jesus, what if he recognizes me from gettin' caught sneakin in!* But he never said anything, so . . . I'm not about to bring it up."

"Is he a dominating force?"

"At first, Bill offered a lot of advice. He never told me what to do or not to do, but he did keep a very close watch on me. But that's okay—he's my *boss*, right? Of course, now that things are goin' so good, he's not around as much. He's around, but he's more or less accepted my success, so he lets me go my own way where possible. I knew from the start that he wasn't goin' to put his ass on the line for me or anyone else, so I had to prove myself first."

His shower finished, Money retreats into the bedroom. He picks out a pinstripe suit to wear for the upcoming show. He dresses as we continue to converse. "I suppose Graham was attracted to the potential commerciality of your stuff," I remark. Both of Money's albums are full of potential hit singles. Each song runs no longer than four minutes and has the taste and texture of late-sixties American rock. His first album produced two hit singles, "Baby Hold On" and "Two Tickets to Paradise"; the second followed with "Maybe I'm a Fool" and "Maureen."

"Well, my background was the Rascals, the Vagrants, James Brown. Ya know, the front man. I've always been into that kinda thing. I thought Felix Cavaliere and Eddie Brigati were great songwriters! I still do. If my songs are potentially commercial, that's fine. As long as I'm not fakin' it, as long as I'm not sacrificing anything, what's wrong? I'm out there to communicate. I feel I can do that in the span of three or four minutes. My band's not gonna do a two-hour Grateful Dead jam in the middle of a song! My music's very important and very personal to me. I have a lot to say, and this is the manner I've chosen to say it."

"So being commercial's not necessarily a sin?"

"Why should it be? I been at this for over ten years. . . . I know music, and I love it. I also know the business. I'm the one who has always kept an ear cocked toward success—it wasn't somethin' that Graham had to instill in me. Most all the moves I've made in my career have been very carefully worked out. I wrote 'Baby Hold On' for the first album with the idea in my head that it would yield me good radio air play. I wanted a hit single—I figured I needed one to somehow separate me from the thirty million other guys who had albums coming out at the same time. I knew the audience I wanted to reach and the manner in which I could reach them. And it worked! 'Two Tickets' was a surprise, although I understand now why that went as a single.

"I followed that up on the second album. It's a much tighter album, 'cause I'm much tighter now, but it's got that *feel* about it that I like. The sound that the two million or so people I've played in front of over the last two years . . . the sound they responded to. You learn a lot out on the road, particularly about your audience. My new album's got some of the best stuff I've ever written on it.

"Me and the band have gotten better. I work with some of

37

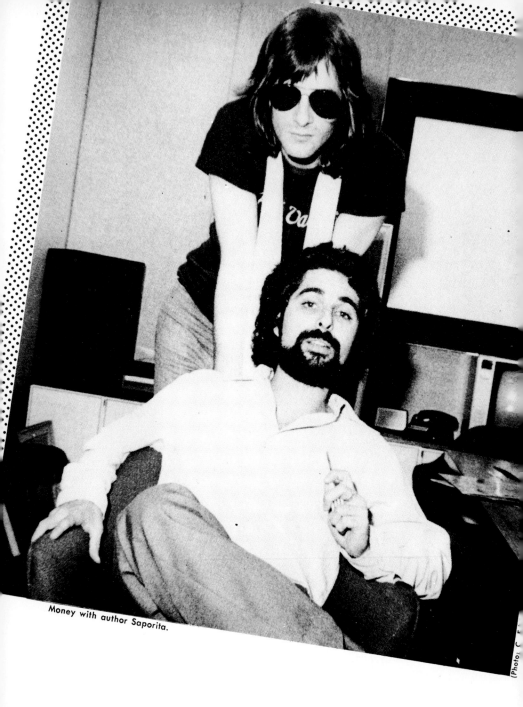

Money with author Saporita.

Steve Miller's cats in the studio, and we've gotten to know each
other better so the whole sound's improved. Shit, most the cuts on the
first album were done in one take! The second album's a little
more polished.

"Hey," Money laughs, "this is gettin' a little too serious. Let's call
room service and get some booze."

The call's made, and a bottle and a bucket of ice are delivered
in minutes. We adjourn to the next room, where Money's band
members are working out preconcert nerves by watching television's
Chuck Barris harangue his "Gong Show" participants.

Money turns the volume down so that he and the band can warm up
acoustically. "Hey, guys," he jokes, "let's not screw up tonight.
My parents are gonna be there!"

The warmup lasts a quarter of an hour. When it's over, Money and
his best friend, lead guitarist Jimmy Lyon, finalize the song list.
It's decided that in addition to the usual set, they'll try out two
brand-new songs. "I think we know them good enough by now,"
Money says. "Anyway, we'll find out."

There's a phone call from Money's manager. He is at the Felt Forum
overseeing the technical details of the evening's performance. He
tells Money that two limousines have been dispatched to bring him
and the band to the Garden. "Whatever you do," he implores,
"don't take the Chevy! I want you to get here in one piece!"

Money hangs up. "Don't take the Chevy," he mutters. "What's the
matter with the guy? Doesn't he have any faith in American
technology? That car's a jewel."

"Maybe he doesn't trust me," the driver suggests, his eyes glassy
from an overload of pot and whiskey.

"Maybe he *shouldn't!*" the band replies in unison.

"Hey," Money grins, "I'll *take* the limo. Shit, I've always wanted to be chauffeured back and forth from a show. I'm not ashamed to admit it. See, that's what it's all about these days. Kids don't wanna grow up to be President—they want to be rock 'n' roll stars! It's like, 'I want a mansion in the hills. . . . I wanna burn thousand-dollar bills.' That's okay! That's American, right?"

Downstairs, two limousines await our unruly entourage. We pile in, beer bottles hidden in the folds of our clothing. Our car pulls away from the curb. I turn around, only to see an unmarked cruiser following us. Christ! Apprehension and anxiety turn my face white. "Hey," Money laughs, noticing my unease. "Is that what's been botherin' you? I told you not to worry. That's my brother! He's comin' to the show!"

The cruiser pulls in front of us, and we are escorted, siren and all, to the Forum's stage door, delivering Money into a sea of young feminine flesh.

(Photo: R. Platzer)

Meat Loaf

MEAT LOAF

The sight is something less than comely: a behemoth figure, growling and grimacing in what appears to be pain, sweating a veritable rainfall, moving across the stage with all the fury of a Southwest twister. Certainly Meat Loaf's mien is the antithesis of rock's implicit sexuality. In a world where tight jeans caressing small buttocks, and sinewy, almost emaciated bodies are revered, Meat Loaf's bulk is an undeniable rarity, made all the more so by the fact that many of his female fans claim him both attractive and desirable. "I think they like the idea of being *surrounded*," laughs Meat Loaf (or Meat, as his fans have come to call him), his voice flecked with the drawl indicative of a childhood spent in Texas.

Meat Loaf's career, thus far, has been phenomenal. On the strength of a single album he has become a major draw throughout the world, playing as many as 170 dates a year to sold-out concert halls and coming away the conquerer at each stop.

Meat's album is *Bat Out of Hell*. Its sales would cause Willy Loman to froth at the mouth—as of January 1980 it went double platinum and then some (close to three million copies sold) in the United States and gold (grossing $1 million in revenues) in Canada and Australia. Europe has followed suit. Total sales, as of spring 1980, are more than five million. Two years since its release, *Bat Out of Hell* still holds a coveted spot on myriad radio stations' playlists.

(In December 1979 Epic Records reported that Meat Loaf and company were halfway into their second album. As this book went to press, the album had not yet been released.)

Meat Loaf (real name, Marvin Lee Aday) confides, "I worked twelve years to get this. I'd hate think of it as a fluke."

The overwhelming success of Meat and company is far from a fluke. Working with composer-songwriter (and close friend) Jim Steinman, Meat Loaf set out to overtake the rock world. Together,

Meat Loaf with partner Jim Steinman.

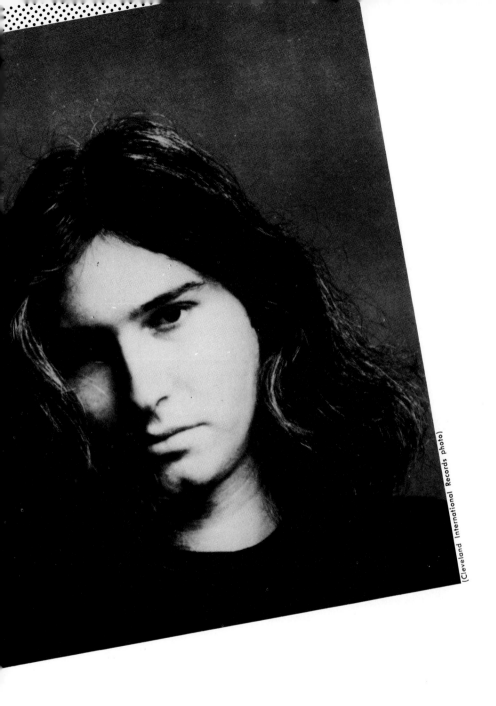

they worked out their game plan for more than a year (rehearsing at New York's Ansonia Hotel) before presenting it to industry A and R men in the hope of procuring a record contract.

"Even then," Meat Loaf recalls, "most of them weren't exactly thrilled with our stuff. They weren't exactly jumping all over themselves to sign us."

Perhaps the companies weren't overimpressed because they smelled "calculated rock"—that is, sensed that Steinman's songs were too formulated, too cliché ridden, and therefore destined to be refuted by the critics as weak parody. But producer-writer-star Todd Rundgren was impressed—so impressed that he offered to produce and play on the pair's debut album. (It was Rundgren's pull within the industry that gradually led the pair to a lucrative contract with Cleveland International, a wing of Epic Records.)

"Once Todd heard us and we talked with him, we were convinced that he had to be in on the making of the album," explains Meat Loaf. "He understood just what we were trying to do."

Partner Steinman is Stan Laurel to Meat Loaf's Oliver Hardy. Steinman is thin and lanky. He's content to let Meat bask in superstardom, preferring to write and compose quietly in the shadow of his gargantuan friend. Steinman is also deadly serious about his work.

He dismisses the oft-mentioned "calculated rock" label with a single blow: "My songs are anthems, anthems to what I consider to be the essence of rock 'n' roll. They have fury, melody, and passion. My songs are rock 'n' roll, period. I believe in the art form. Like Peter Pan's Never Never Land, rock is a convenient place not to grow up. Which is the ultimate teenage fantasy. The album cover [a burning-red sketch of a motorcyclist bursting out of a graveyard] shows all that—the crashing out of the graveyard, defying the

(Photo: R. Platzer)

The Loaf on the mound.

adult world, and ultimately defying death.''

If all this sounds a bit theatrical, particularly for rock 'n' roll, it is because both Steinman and Meat Loaf share a prestigious theatrical background. Steinman was brought to Manhattan by the Shakespeare Festival's director, Joseph Papp, who saw Steinman as a promising young playwright. Meat was performing for Papp, and he played a small role in the devastatingly absurd cult film *The Rocky Horror Picture Show*.

The two became friends when both took a gig with the *National Lampoon Road Show*. During the tour, Steinman introduced Meat Loaf to some of the songs he'd been writing, songs that are now the core of *Bat Out of Hell*. ''I wasn't sure Meat's *voice* (a booming, gut-conceived, esophagus-destroying yowl) was right for rock 'n' roll,'' Steinman laughs. ''I figured he might be better off singing opera or something. But it seems to have worked out.''

Watching Meat Loaf and Steinman on stage, backed by a solid band, is a study in the team's dichotomy—Meat is afire, generating such force from his mass that it appears the entire stage may collapse, whereas Steinman is at ease behind his piano, playing almost lethargically.

Meat's performance is so furious that at the end of every show he has taken to inhaling pure oxygen from a tank ready in the wings. As the show ends he is supraheated jelly, barely able to catch his breath. Steinman, on the other hand, fields a question from a reporter the moment he leaves the stage. It is the now-typical question concerning the subject matter of his songs.

''Look,'' Steinman explains with some annoyance, as if the nonstop screaming of twenty thousand fans really needs to be explained. ''Okay, you're seventeen. Something's been building up inside you, and suddenly it explodes. Then it begins to fade away; you're

Greeting the public.

growing older, and you don't like it. Rock 'n' roll, to me, is the perfect way to hold on to the moment *before* that explosion, the moment of being forever young. That's what it's all about.''

''Yeah,'' adds his partner, a final hit from the oxygen tank conveying pure life into his veins, ''I think everybody's got a kid deep down inside him, a child who wishes he'd never gotten old. And Jim's very good at expressing that kind of thing.''

A roadie comes into the room with the news that the audience is still on its feet, well into a ten-minute ovation.

The band agrees on an encore. On his rush to the stage, Meat is accosted by two slim blond females. One is content to run her hands along his sides. The other has him in a Masked Marvel hold, pushing her mons veneris deep into his crotch. Meat breaks loose, yelping in glee as the girl pinches his ass. ''One thing I forgot to mention,'' he beams. ''Whether you take this shit seriously or not—it sure beats the hell out of workin'!''

49

Van Morrison

(Warner Bros. Records photo)

VAN MORRISON

The small man's receding hairline and slight paunch reveal the fifteen years that have passed since he first began his long seduction of the muse. He was the "wrong" side of twenty years old when, as lead singer of the group Them, he wrote his first hit. The song was "Gloria"—a paean to the pain-pleasure of unrequited adolescent yearnings. His long hair hung straight to his shoulders. His vocal delivery was unique; he was a poet, a storyteller who chose to work with both words and music, not unlike the Gaelic bards whose lineage he shares.

He is an enigma. His compositions are the most intelligent, most insightful, most personal in the business; yet in interviews he is frustratingly noncommittal, almost inarticulate. He is an introvert, unconvinced of his extraordinary talent. His stage fright is legendary; yet once on stage he becomes a man obsessed, actually infused, with the music; his concerts are unexcelled.

Van's been a rhythm-and-blues aficionado since early childhood. He is one of the few white musicians who can cover classics like "Bring It on Home," "Help Me," and "Ain't Nothin' You Can Do" with the same passion that their creators, the early bluesmen, can. His own soul fire, prominent in "Brown-eyed Girl," "Caravan," "Tupelo Honey," "Wavelength," and "When the Healing Has Begun," has earned him the nickname Van the Man.

Nowhere is the source of the moniker more evident than in performance. Deep into a blistering instrumental, Van turns toward his nine-piece band and with a quick whip of his right arm brings them to near silence. He pauses, keeping the band at a whisper volume for sixteen bars; then he pours out, *"Turn it up!"* and the entire band blams back into the tune, wailing it at full force.

More a conductor than a performer, Van draws the band far into themselves, trading leads from instrument to instrument with his

Van Morrison

scat-like vocal delivery. It is a technique both admired and emulated by many of the younger stars, including Springsteen, Billy Joel, Graham Parker, Thin Lizzy, and Eddie Money.

But that is not to say that the youngsters have reached their master's plateau. As Eddie Money so aptly remarked, "There is only one Van the Man. There will never be another."

(Warner Bros. Records photo)

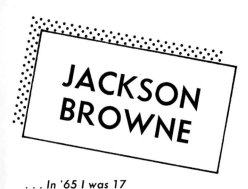

JACKSON BROWNE

. . . In '65 I was 17
runnin' up 101
in '69 I was 21
and I called the road my own
I don't know when that road turned onto the road I'm on
  "Runnin' on Empty"
  Jackson Browne

Most of us recall high school as the last time we could be completely frivolous—the last long laugh at the world before the final commitment of making it on our own. Sure, there were certain pressures—working hard to make good grades, frightened that without them we wouldn't get accepted at college or get a good job; struggling for a spot on the athletic team; pursuing the one heartthrob that was always just out of reach—but these pressures seemed somehow trivial, coming only in brief spurts.

What really mattered was who hung out with whom, who was going steady, and what was up for the weekend. Secure in our parents' homes and among our contemporaries, we looked on the outside world as a far-off, senseless mass of confusion, something to be laughed at, to be scorned.

There would be plenty of time to worry about money, marriage, and all the rest. With all our young wisdom—that singular mixture of naïveté and bravado—we felt sure that when the time came we would be able to breeze our way through the realities of adulthood as easily, and in exactly the same manner, as we had through school years.

But young wisdom, like most visions born of innocence, is a bit short-sighted. Not long after graduation, we began to perceive that surviving as an adult is an extremely arduous task, involving both intelligence and cunning. Had most of us attempted that universal obstacle course armed only with the rose-colored glasses of youth, we would have been crushed.

Jackson Browne

Now consider this: At age seventeen, no older than a high school senior, Jackson Browne was already being touted as one of the finest songwriters to emerge in a long while. At an age when most of his peers were still worried about their final grades, Browne found himself a welcome guest among rock's elite. A lucrative recording contract and subsequent career were not far off.

That was fourteen years ago. At thirty-one, the still-young artist has five accomplished albums to his credit and a lifetime ahead of him.

(Photo: R. St. Nicholas)

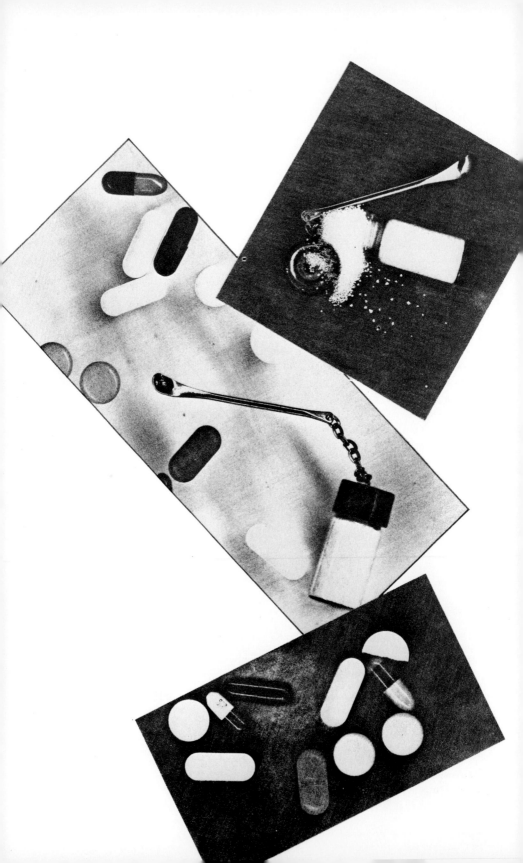

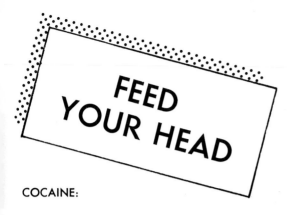

FEED YOUR HEAD

COCAINE:

The way to a rock star's heart is through his or her nose. Cocaine is *the* preferred high. Very expensive; anywhere from one thousand to two thousand dollars an ounce. Nonetheless, the wealthier stars always have a decent quantity on hand. An excellent stimulant, with a euphoric kick comparable to an ongoing orgasm, coke is generally used to break the doldrums of, say, a five-month, six-shows-five-cities-a-week national tour. A few thick lines snorted moments before going onstage, and the long, weary hours and days of traveling, hotel food, sound checks, and so forth, are soon forgotten. One becomes supercharged, the only thoughts alive at that moment, those concerning the upcoming performance.

Especially loved by roadies—the work crews who set up and break down the equipment at each gig and are responsible for transporting the equipment from city to city. During a major tour, roadies are usually at work seventeen hours a day. To a roadie, good coke is not only pleasurable; it is a godsend.

POT:

There is virtually no one in the industry who doesn't smoke pot now or hasn't at one time. Grass is so prevalent that quality runs the gamut from awful (producing a headache instead of a high) to psyche-splitting. Some of the more potent varieties include Hawaiian, Columbian gold, Kona gold, toreeon, and Sinsemilla.

Use within the music business can be traced back to the jazz world and the late twenties. Cab Calloway, Duke Ellington, Bessie Smith, and Billie Holiday all sang the praises of cannabis. Calloway's "The Reefer Man" was a widespread "underground" hit at the time.

Once, pot was touted as a great creative stimulus. It is evident, for instance, that the rock 'n' roll of the late sixties (culminating at the Woodstock Festival in 1969) was highly influenced by pot.

There was something new about the high back then—for young white kids anyway—that is reflected in the music. See early Grateful Dead, Jefferson Airplane, Doors, Hendrix, and Byrds material for references.

Pot can still act as a muse inducer, but for the most part it is smoked in much the same manner that beer is drunk—as a good, quick, relatively cheap high.

And you can see me tonight with an illegal smile
it don't cost very much but it lasts a long while
Won't you please tell the Man I didn't kill anyone
No I'm just trying to have some fun
   "Illegal Smile"
   J. Prine

ALCOHOL:

For the most part, booze has been replaced by pot or coke. The big drinkers of the past have either died or taken the cure. Pigpen (Grateful Dead organist and lead singer) is dead. So are Janis Joplin and Hendrix. Joe Cocker came close to death, quit, now drinks moderately. Alice Cooper (who drank a case and a half of beer a day for years) checked himself into a sanitorium a few years back to kick the habit. He drinks milk on the road now. Kris Kristofferson quit in 1977; until then he had *never* appeared before an audience straight.

Some of the punks are heavy drinkers; some consume almost *anything* that contains alcohol, but that's probably because (1) for the most part they are younger than the huge stars and therefore haven't been drinking long enough to develop the symptoms of alcoholism; and (2) they don't make as much money as the others, and in the long run, alcohol is a cheaper high than, say, pot or coke.

Most of the groups' contracts contain riders specifying the alcohol that is to be on hand backstage. Beer (almost always imported) is a top priority, if only as a thirst quencher. The odd bottles of Scotch, vodka, and whiskey are also requested. There are special

60

demands: Dylan likes choice, vintage wines. The Stones and Rod Stewart have a certain affection for expensive aged brandy.

Rita Coolidge, ex-wife of Kristofferson, responding to a question concerning Kris's swearing-off of the bottle: "It's very nice now to get up in the morning and not have to make a few drinks first thing."

QUAALUDES:

"Sopors" are both a powerful aphrodisiac and a strong sleep inducer. Almost never used onstage—the performance would invariably be sloppy, if not a complete flop. Quaaludes are usually saved for post-concert celebrations and such. A black market has sprung up but the questionable quality of bootleg ludes has made caution necessary.

METHAMPHETAMINE; METHEDRINE:

In the past half-decade, speed has taken a back seat to cocaine. Coke's high is quick and clean; "doing speed" can mean a full day (or more) of being wired. Most of the true speed freaks (they usually inject it into a vein) have long since burned out. Those who are still around keep it well hidden.

Speed kills.
—Steve Gibbons, Steve Gibbons Band

HEROIN:

A very touchy subject. Some of those who have admitted addiction: Duane Allman (dead), Janis Joplin (dead), Johnny Winter (took the cure), Eric Clapton (also took the cure).

When he was with the Velvet Underground, Lou Reed wrote a celebrated song called "Heroin." He has never publicly said anything further about the matter. Dylanologist A. J. Weberman insists that every time Dylan writes about horses, it is an allusion to heroin (*horse, smack,* and *junk* are all popular slang for heroin).

61

Dylan has never bothered to comment on Weberman's statements.

I got into smack because it was an escape. You see, I'd walk down the street, go to a restaurant, or what have you, and people were always coming up to me asking me for my autograph or whatever. I was never alone. So I'd go home, shoot up, and suddenly all that bullshit was gone. I was myself again. You see, I had to get that high to get back to reality.
   —Johnny Winter

MESCALINE, PSILOCYBIN, PEYOTE, ACID (LSD):

The hallucinogens; their use is mostly recreational. Tripping and performing don't usually go hand in hand (the high is too unreliable), although at one time (circa 1965) bands like the Grateful Dead and the Jefferson Airplane certainly did play under the influence. It was all one huge experiment back then, a probe into just exactly how psychedelics could affect the manner in which one approached one's music.

Their use was precipitated by author Ken Kesey's (*One Flew over the Cuckoo's Nest*) Trips Festivals.

For better or for worse, the use of hallucinogens has steadily decreased since the mid-seventies.

There was a time when we'd try and dose just about the whole audience. We had the Kool-Aid, Owsley cooked up a nice bunch of acid, and we'd pass the stuff around. Of course, we always told people—we never wanted to fuck anybody up who didn't know about it. But that was a long time ago, the vibes were a lot different. Couldn't get away with it any more.
   —An unidentified member of the Grateful Dead entourage.

NITROUS OXIDE; WHIPPETS:

"I'm sorry, I can't hear you. I've got a balloon in my mouth."
Conventional use of nitrous is in a dentist's office. When a dentist gives gas as a painkiller, she or he is administering nitrous oxide.

64

A debilitating high. Nitrous has an ethereal quality, as if the user is floating far above his or her body.

Tanks of nitrous (huge, four-foot-high cylinders weighing a few hundred pounds) have found their way out of dentists' offices and into backstage dressing rooms on more than a few occasions.

To use it, one attaches an empty balloon to the tank's aperture and fills the balloon with gas, then takes hits from the balloon.

This can be a very dangerous high. More than one person has died from using nitrous, because it's relatively easy to inhale too much gas with too little oxygen.

AMYL NITRATE (POPPER):

Heart medicine, a powerful punch when a capsule is broken directly beneath the nose and the fumes are inhaled. Since amyl nitrate is now a prescription drug, a chemical relative, butyl nitrite, is often used. Butyl can be bought in "poppers" or in small bottles.

Not much use in rock 'n' roll; favored by the disco crowd.

DOWNS (PERCODANS, SECONAL, TUINAL, VALIUM, DALMANE):

A step away from Quaaludes (read not as powerful), downs are readily available, but if anything, use has decreased lately.

Used occasionally at parties.

CARBONA (SPOT REMOVER); GLUE:

One of the oldest, cheapest highs. *Extremely* dangerous. The high is achieved simply by inhaling the fumes. A major preference of many of the punks.

SUGGESTED READING:

Physicians Desk Reference (PDR); *High Times* magazine

Blondie

PUNK

In a September 1961 interview author Henry Miller defined Dada, the highly unconventional art movement of the twenties, as "a deliberate, conscious effort to turn the tables upside-down, to show the absolute insanity of present-day life, the worthlessness of all our values."

Miller might just as well have been defining punk rock. In many ways punk is the grandchild of Dada. Like Dada, punk began as an open protest against the more established art form—in this case, punk rallied against the commercialization of rock 'n' roll, against the multimillion-dollar industry it had become. What better way to express displeasure than, as Miller put it, to "turn the tables upside-down"?

Punks are proud of their rough edges. Many of them are dismal musicians, but they couldn't care less. If all they can manage are three chords, at least those chords are played with some fervor and not with the bland, smooth-as-silk, sounds-exactly-like-the-record performances of the wealthy, often jaded superstars.

Punks enjoy the precipice of dangerous, or at least potentially dangerous, behavior. Rock stars indulge in dope with some caution. Punks deliberately set out to get "fucked up." The stars admire and appreciate their audiences. Punks feel that the audience deserves all the respect that they themselves are worthy of—that is, none. The most outrageous of the acts (the defunct Sex Pistols, the Contortions, the Dictators, Teenage Jesus and the Jerks) abuse their fans both verbally and physically. Again, like the Dada artists before them, the punks are setting out to deliberately "show the worthlessness of all our values."

In this case, the values being challenged are those which lead legions of fans to raise their idols onto towering pedestals. Punks almost beg to be disliked; an excellent evening's performance is one in which some member of the audience has been properly

(Photo: B. Fitzgerald)

Suzy Creamcheese goes punk.

flogged—verbally more often than not, although at times hard-nosed fisticuffs have broken out between the bands and the fans.

The beginning of punk can be traced back to New York's Lower East Side, the late spring of 1975, within a dingy broken-down Bowery bar named CBGB & OMFUG (abbreviated to CBGB's). Proprietor Hilly Kristal (now a full-fledged punk impresario) explains, "The bands found me, really. I guess I was the first to give them a stage to play on. I didn't think that much of it, although it did occur to me that they were certainly different than your run-of-the-mill rock band."

Three names come to mind: Patti Smith, Richard Hell, and the Ramones. Patti had already gained a good deal of attention (and notoriety) as a new-age poet, an avant-garde extension of the best of the beat poets. When she hooked up with guitarist and rock critic Lenny Kaye—Kaye strumming his guitar alongside her as she spat out her poems—she succeeded in doing what Kerouac before her had attempted: marrying music and poetry. Kerouac used jazz. Patti and Lenny combined to produce what was later defined as three-chord rock: a kind of immature, almost naive, certainly unstructured sound. It was a new form, providing a wall of sound upon which Patti could hang her poetry, often stretching the words into musical notes.

Whatever else it was, it was punk. Let's just say that at the start Patti and Lenny weren't exactly harmonious. Yet they persevered, through catcalls and jeers, convinced that they were working out a new art form. (Five years later, it seems they were right. Patti and Lenny—now expanded into the Patti Smith group—are among a handful of punks still performing.)

The Ramones invaded CBGB's with a force overcome initially only by their lack of talent. Their first few times onstage were laudable only for the sheer guts they brought with them. In 1975, I don't think any of the Ramones knew more than four chords, all major.

Patti Smith

(Photo: J. Presler)

Joey Ramone. His face had been burned severely backstage; yet he refused to cancel the performance. Immediately following the concert, he was hospitalized with extensive second and third-degree burns.

(Photo: C. Frick)

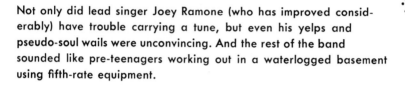

Not only did lead singer Joey Ramone (who has improved consid-
erably) have trouble carrying a tune, but even his yelps and
pseudo-soul wails were unconvincing. And the rest of the band
sounded like pre-teenagers working out in a waterlogged basement
using fifth-rate equipment.

What the Ramones lacked in talent they compensated for with an
overflowing well of energy. The ferocity of their sound alone
garnered them an audience (punks are notoriously happy when the
music reaches a level where all thought is drowned out). It soon
became apparent that a sardonic sense of humor lurked beneath
their screeching blanket of noise. Some of the Ramones' more
popular songs include "Loudmouth," "Blitzkrieg Bop," "Carbona
(Not Glue)," and "I Wanna Be Sedated." They, too, have persevered
(with a change in drummers), and most critics agree they have
improved greatly. They are the best-known of the punk bands.

Richard Hell (and The Voidoids) came up with the first real
definition of punk rock. Hell's composition "Blank Generation"
(chorus: "We are all a blank generation") became the punk anthem.
Although many fans may have misunderstood Hell's cry, thinking
blank meant devoid of any thought, Hell explained to critic Lester
Bangs: "By blank, I mean we have wiped away everything that
came before us. So we are blank, an empty canvas. And we are
free to create something entirely new on that blank canvas."

Britain's punk scene rose on the heels of America's with one important
difference—the punk scene in Britain is much more politically
inclined. Consisting mostly of England's lower class, the punks have
chosen their music as the vehicle for social protest—actually an
outcry against the rapidly deteriorating status of the Commonwealth.
High Times magazine writer Victor Bockris reported the following
explanation from one of London's rock critics: "Americans don't
understand English punk at all because the English punk audience
is much younger (15–18) and they're all truly frustrated, bitter kids
who have to get drunk very quickly in order to have a good time.

(Photo: C. DeAlmeida)

Punkster Crayola.

(Photo: C. DeAlmeida)

Victim's bass player
pays tribute to the
Hot Rods.

Talking Head's lead man, former art student David Byrne.

Talking Head Tina Weymouth.

Heartbreaker's Lure on stage.

Dressed to kill—bass player for the Misfits.

(Photo: C. DeAlmeida)

English punks are totally committed to punk rock and don't see it as an amusement but a cause."

The best of England's punks—the Clash, the Damned, Ian Dury and the Blockheads, Sham 69—reflect the lower class's discontent with English society, following in the well-worn path that Johnny Rotten ("Anarchy in the U.K.") and his Sex Pistols blazed until they split in 1978.

THE CLOTHING:

Punk attire is a simple extension of the punk lifestyle, or punkitude (as in attitude). As the artists deliberately set out to disrupt contemporary rock-music mores, so they also deliberately set out to outrage everyone by their appearance. The least offensive just don't care what they wear; in other words, they wear the same clothing onstage as off, usually consisting of ripped jeans and tattered T-shirts.

The more outlandish of the pack decorate themselves with ornaments never intended for the human body. Safety pins as earrings have become the punk trademark, but the dress of some bands far surpasses what has become such commonplace craziness. There are young men and women living in Manhattan and London whose body hair is all dyed purple. One woman lead singer's nipples are pierced by fourteen-karat-gold safety pins. Another has grown the hair beneath her armpits long enough to be worn in braids. During the summer of 1979, in CBGB's men's room, I watched a punk star (who vanished from the scene shortly thereafter and is presumed dead) slash his abdomen with a broken bottle. As he went onstage, the audience watched, enthralled, as the wound bled, then began to clot. He tore at the clot, spewing fresh pieces of scab onto young female onlookers.

76

Cheetah Chrome, former Dead Boy, resembles the final remnant of some long-lost alien race. Johnny Rotten (real name John Lydon), who gained his nickname from the fact that he hasn't brushed his teeth since the early 1970s, dresses like Cheetah's deformed brother. It is all part of a concentrated effort to drive the mainstream of society mad with hatred and disgust. Of course, in that way, it also forces the mainstream to come to grips with its innate and not so innate prejudices.

THE SURVIVORS

As we move into the eighties, punk appears to be dying out. A simple explanation would be that a force so devastating, so bent on destruction, so inherently self-annihilating could not last longer than a half decade. If your lifestyle consists of the absolute denial of any sort of lifestyle, you will eventually cease to exist.

For the most part, that is precisely what happened to punk— it came, it mocked, it conquered, and finally, it blew itself apart. Yet punk also left in its wake a group of survivors—a group who, ultimately, became survivors by assimilation. They followed in the footsteps of the rock stars they once disdained—signing profitable record contracts, embarking on huge national tours, becoming involved with the record industry, and so on. To state it simply, they sold out. Patti Smith, The Ramones, Talking Heads, Blondie (whose 1979 "Heart of Glass" was a *worldwide* hit), the Dictators, Tom Verlaine, Robert Gordon (an original Tuff Darts member), and Richard Hell are all survivors.

And as might be expected, each new record by any of the above is a step further from the original intentions of punk.

Sid Vicious at Max's Kansas City. A month later he was dead of a heroin overdose.

(Photo: C. DeAlmeida)

THE PROPER LAMENT FOR THE PREMIER PUNK

On February 20, 1979, less than a month after he had awakened on a bitter cold morning to find his girlfriend lying beside him dead from multiple stab wounds, Sid Vicious succumbed to a heroin overdose.

What came as a surprise when Vicious chose to hurl himself into eternity was not so much the act as the reaction to it. Suddenly Sid became a martyr.

What nonsense!

The cat didn't want to be sainted or hallowed; he didn't even want to be remembered. *Dis*membered—figuratively, of course—would have suited him better. Face it, the guy couldn't play the bass, couldn't sing, knew almost nothing about music, and lacked even the slightest hint of charisma.

Great. That's how he and his fellow Sex Pistols planned it all along. Less than zero catapulted into greatness. The ultimate mock. Vicious and his cohorts were so rude, so outrageous, so vile to their audiences that they literally begged to be despised. Of course, they were loved by the press and the public alike.

So at age twenty-one, Vicious died of his excesses. No death goes unnoticed, nor does any lifetime, no matter how brief. Vicious was an extreme. Extremes never last; they burn intensely, then snuff. Witness Hendrix, Morrison, and Joplin. This is not to say that Vicious equaled any of them in talent, but he did equal their intensity, their effect on the people who watched and listened to them.

The Sex Pistols invaded our consciousness for a fleeting yet smoldering moment. They split up and Sid died. Want to really do right by the man? Laugh aloud at his demise. Celebrate. Have a drink (better yet, get disgustingly drunk) in his memory. Desecrate his tomb.

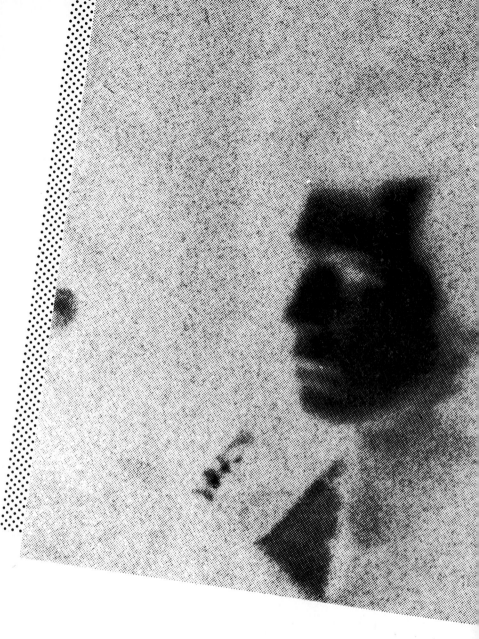

If that sounds horrible to you, you've missed the whole point of Sid's life. All that exhibitionism was designed to make us take a very serious look at ourselves. At what we believe in, at our reverence for materialism, at our multiple-sins society.

Admit to your own dark side. Exorcise it in Sid's name. You couldn't do better by him.

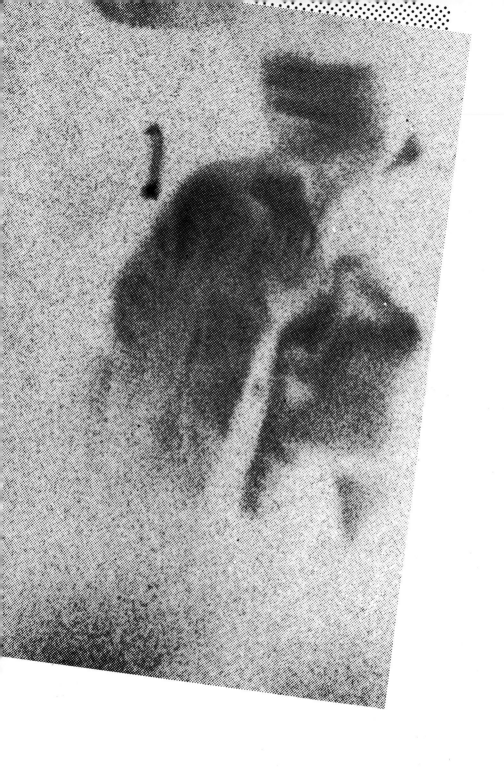

(Photo: C. DeAlmeida)

NUKE'EM T
GLC

Dee Dee Ramone

BACKSTAGE WAVE

Passaic's Capitol Theatre—It was bad enough that Eddie and his Hot Rods were set up in the prime dressing room, the luxurious suite with the fully equipped bathroom (shower and all), beautiful thick shag rug, and brand-new comfortable couches, but there they were, not twenty yards from Dee Dee Ramone, and Eddie's bass player was using Dee's amplifier as a receptacle for his onstage fanaticism. This guy was ripping the hell out of Dee Dee's amp, and there was not a thing Dee could do but watch from his dressing-room window, which afforded him a clear view of the stage, and pray to CBGB's that Eddie's rocker didn't destroy the thing beyond recognition.

"What the hell's he doing?" Dee kept muttering. Not that the young woman with the fire-engine-red hair sitting next to Dee cared. She might not have even *understood* his anger, but she reassured him time and again that it would be all right and that, in time, all would be fine. She ran a very pale hand up and down Dee's crotch, digging pink nails along the top teeth of his zipper. Dee just shrugged, strapped on his bass, plugged it into a small preamp, and began a drone that didn't stop until the the Ramones were ushered onstage two hours later.

The Rods, meanwhile, kicked out a mean jam (Eddie barechested and sweating like a boiler-room worker) and left the stage in a fury of punk mania. Now Eddie and his boys, all proper English chaps and full of fun, just couldn't resist a touch of pranksterism. Sure, there were tubs filled with cans of beer (most of which had already been consumed or secreted away in their touring bus parked outside), more than a few half-empty bottles of bourbon, and other nefarious (and illegal) things floating around—so maybe some nonsense was inevitable. But try telling the Capitol's cleanup crew that. Eddie and the guys decided the best way to dispose of the huge bowls of salad left over from a complete preshow steak dinner was to grace the dressing room with a torrential precipitation of lettuce, sliced tomatoes, and chopped onions. The walls and the carpet became a wide field of vegetables, both dormant and flying.

Then the lead guitarist figured that a beer shampoo would be best to clean the heavily damaged carpet. He urged his comrades to join him, and together they flooded the floor, the beer splashing against furniture, walls, and guests.

John Scher, the Capitol's proprietor, arrived ten minutes later, surveyed the damage, and shrugged the massacre off with a definitive statement to the the Hot Rod's manager: "That's okay—we needed some new furniture anyway."

When the manager expressed his consternation to Scher, denying that his people were the perpetrators, a battle of words ensued. The language became so vicious and vile it would have caused sailors to cower. Scher emerged the victor. It .was agreed that the necessary repairs would be paid for by the Rods.

Tuff Darts (who had opened the evening's festivities) missed the whole fiasco. They were across the hall, tucked away in a broom closet that had been cleaned and outfitted as a dressing room. But they, too, were in a joyous mood. Their performance that evening had been met with a hearty response, and their manager had informed them earlier that a contract deal had gone through and they were now officially on Sire records. They sat drinking from a bottle of Johnnie Walker Red.

Tuff Darts' lead singer Tommy Q. Public became involved in a discussion with a friend as to the merits of various hair products. Tommy preferred Groom and Clean, he confided. "I like to use at least a tubeful a show," he bragged, grabbing a sheaf of hair and coming up with a hand shimmering with gunk. "You should see my pillowcases! I think the stain and the smell has scared off more chicks than the sight of me naked!"

(Photo: C. DeAlmeida)

Johnny Ramone

"Yeah," his friend answered. "I believe it. And that's a sight I wouldn't wish on anyone. To me, there's nothing that works better than Score and baby oil. It's really great, 'cause the baby oil drips down on your face and in the lights on stage it makes it look like you're sweatin' your ass off. The audience really gets off on that!"

"Truthfully," Public interrupted, "the best product I've found so far is Koromex [contraceptive jelly, used with diaphragms]. It not only flattens down the hair good, but it's a good thing to have along with you anyway."

Back at the Ramones' dressing room, confusion reigned as showtime neared. A trio of fans, women so strange, alien sirens made up in a distorted emulation of Picasso's severest abstractions, huddled near the group. One lady, who sneered to a reporter, "My name's Dawn, you creep," surrounded Dee Dee, attempting, it seemed, not only to pull his attention away from his warmup drone, but to separate his very flesh from his bones. She was pulling at him with all the intensity of a child keeping his or her favorite toy from another kid.

Joey, the torn-blue-jeaned, slim-as-a-stick vocalist, was suffering from a cold that had left his sinuses crammed full of mucus. Even Joey's banal braying, a purposeful monotone that has become his signature, could not survive stuffed nasal passages. So the dressing room was cleared, and preparations were begun to ease Joey's ailment. Vicks hadn't worked, nor had a double dosage of Dristan. "We gotta do somethin'," Joey moaned. "We go on in a few minutes."

A sidekick decided that a metal teapot equipped with a long, slender metal tube would make the perfect ersatz vaporizer. The teapot was filled with water and set on a hotplate to heat. When the water began to boil vigorously, the pipe was inserted in the spout,

86

and Joey was told to bend his head to the pipe's aperture, to snort in nose-clearing clouds of steam.

No one realized that the water, contained as it was by the kettle and pipe, was under tremendous pressure. As Joey bent to the superheated apparatus, there was a screaming explosion, and America's number-one punk found himself with a face full of 200-degree-plus water, blasted onto his flesh.

He screamed, tumbling to the floor in pain. It hurt, a lot, and Ramone was rushed to a nearby hospital. He returned, his face a pure white mass of salve, and the Ramones proceeded to play—an abbreviated set, but they played.

Joey was later hospitalized with first- and second-degree facial burns. Doctors advised a short hospital stay. No matter; he had gone on with the show, proving he was a trouper and proving, further, his punkdom. That night at the Capitol was Ramone's initiation; he had become, indisputably, punk's first real hero.

Costello

ELVIS COSTELLO

I never saw Buddy Holly perform live, but somehow the gaunt frame and gawky appearance of this young man—the obtrusive black-framed glasses, owlish on a Christopher Robin face—coupled with an obvious gift for writing songs that rivals most contemporaries, evokes an image of what Holly must have been like: uniquely talented but glaringly out of place among the glittering personae of his peers.

His real name isn't Elvis, of course (it's Declan Patrick McManus), but the nickname fits well, for Costello comes off as the kind of tough-kid-become-rock-'n'-roller that the real Elvis portrayed in *Jailhouse Rock*. However, Costello's anger plunges far deeper than youthful, rebel-without-a-cause dissent. A former computer operator in an Elizabeth Arden factory in England, he writes wrathful lyrics that reflect the anxieties and fears of the young members of Great Britain's working class.

As the empire has dissolved, the popularity (and power) of the neo-Nazi National Front party has risen. Young Americans visiting England (London, in particular) report that the country is ripe for the racist thought patterns espoused by the National Front. It is a frighteningly familiar pattern: A once-powerful country finds that its prestige, economy, and pride are crumbling. Under the guise of "restoring the empire," the proponents of fascism are picking up followers at an alarming rate.

If this seems too complicated an issue for a rock singer to involve himself with, one would do better to consider Costello a "political artist" who has chosen rock 'n' roll as his vehicle. His lyrics are the most penetrating, most caustic, most intelligent I have heard since the very early days of Dylan.

He has released four albums. The third, *Armed Forces*, is an intense political statement. The fourth, *Get Happy*, is a perfect blend of cynicism, self-mockery, and satire. On his recent world tour, he

came off more like a radical world ambassador—calling attention
to what he perceives to be the upsurge of international fascism—
than an entertainer.

He is certainly no easy interview. His antipathy for the press is
well-known; colleagues have been ejected from his dressing rooms
with no small show of force. At one opening-night performance,
he was reportedly seen carrying a guest list of presspersons,
crossing out the names of all those he felt had dealt him dirt
in the past.

It is rumored that he carries a small black notebook with him that
is fat with the names of people toward whom he can't wait to be
extremely uncharitable. In an industry where it is not unusual to
kowtow to someone who, minutes before, you had wished the
worst curse upon, Elvis Costello is truly unique.

He does not seem comfortable answering questions. One immediately
gets the impression he'd rather be posing the queries. His face
remains featureless, blank, as if he is not listening; yet his answers
are sharp, insightful, and occasionally brutal.

Consenting to an interview, he sits with a notebook, opened to a
blank page, on his lap. Every few minutes he jots *something* down
in a heavy black scrawl. If asked what he's writing, he pauses,
considers his questioner, and continues to scribble. One feels
intimidated; yet for the first time, one understands precisely how a
personality feels when a reporter faces him or her equipped with
an arsenal built of pen, notebook, and tape recorder.

The conversation with him follows.

J.S.:
In retrospect, it seems ironical that your first popular song was
"Alison," a love song, while just recently you remarked that you
didn't really know anything about love.

90

E.C. [*laughs*]:
I don't want to hear another word about young lovers. I wouldn't say that I was raised on romance, but let's not get stuck in the past.

J.S.:
There has been a gradual progression of cynicism in your work. I mean to say, from *My Aim Is True* to *Armed Forces* is quite a leap.

E.C.:
Well, I'd do anything to confuse the enemy. My career is information, and I don't want to be a goody-goody. Some of my friends sit around every evening and worry about the times ahead, but everybody else is overwhelmed by indifference. They're trying to anesthetize the way that we feel.

J.S.:
And?

E.C.:
They'll never end up makin' a lampshade out of me.

J.S.:
Yet you are a part of the industry, you do make albums, you do make money. . . .

E.C.:
I want to bite the hand that feeds me. I want to make them wish they'd never seen me.

J.S.:
Is the outlook that bad?

E.C.:
They really think we're getting out of control. Everybody is under suspicion . . . but you don't want to hear about that.

J.S.:
I'm listening.

E.C.:

I don't know where to begin. *Everything*'s so provocative. You better cut out all identifying labels before they put you on the torture table.

J.S.:

Is it that bad?

E.C.:

Are *you* ready for the final solution?

J.S.:

Of course not. But I'm not sure that, in general, things have deteriorated to that extent.

E.C.:

Sometimes I wonder if we're living in the same land. Okay, you been warned. No uniform's gonna keep you warm. It only takes one itchy trigger.

J.S.:

Can you elaborate on that?

E.C.:

I got a *lot* to say, and I'm not joking. But there are words they don't allow to be spoken.

J.S.:

I wonder how the record-company executives react to those kinds of statements.

E.C.:

I never said I was a diplomat.

J.S.:

This might be as good a time as any to bring up the Bonnie Bramlett incident. [In the midst of his 1979 world tour, Bramlett accused Costello of spouting racist remarks at a post-concert gathering. Fisticuffs ensued; Bramlett managed to dislocate Elvis's shoulder.] It seems ironical that you would be called a racist.

Costello on his first trip to the States.

E.C.:
I'm *not* a racist. Sometimes I wish I could stop them from talking when I hear the silly things they say. But . . . don't ask me to apologize; I won't ask you to forgive me. I'm not angry any more.

J.S.:
Tom Robinson remarked that the whole incident came down to the point that if one is truly nonprejudicial, then one can get away with epithets simply because they become just words, nothing more or less. Kind of like the Lenny Bruce syndrome.

E.C.:
It's the words that we don't say that scare me so. But . . . I'm always hiding from a scandal in the national press.

J.S.:
It does seem that the press, the rock press anyway, are eagerly awaiting a trip-up or something from you. Perhaps it is because you don't exactly cater to them.

E.C.:
I knew right from the start that we'd end up hating. They think that I got no respect, but everything means less than zero.

J.S.:
Doesn't it follow that good press will increase your popularity, and thereby your message will get across to more people?

E.C. [*laughs*]:
I need my head examined.

J.S.:
The idea of press relations doesn't interest you?

E.C.:
I never thought so much trouble was resting on my reply.

(Photo: C. Frick)

Elvis Costello

J.S.:
Well . . .

E.C.:
Look, we could talk and talk until we talk ourselves out of it, but I don't want to chitter-chat.

J.S.:
It comes down to whether or not your absence from the press is intentional.

E.C.:
I know what I've done.

J.S.:
John Rockwell of the *New York Times* once called your wrath and anger "close to clinical."

E.C.:
You say I got no feelings—this is a good time to kill them.

J.S.:
Blame it on John; don't blame it on me.

E.C.:
Sometimes I think I'm going insane from talking to myself for so long.

J.S.:
I take it Rockwell's remark doesn't thrill you.

E.C.:
Every single time I feel a little stronger they tell me it's a crime. Don't you think I know that walking on the water won't make me a miracle man?

J.S.:
So we're back to the press versus Elvis Costello.

E.C.:
You never know when it's a real attraction. I don't want to be hung up or strung up. Or be worrying about the consequences.

J.S.:
Can music be used as a political force?

E.C.:
You better listen to your radio. Those disco synthesizers . . . those daily tranquilizers.

J.S.:
The antithesis of what Elvis Costello's attempting with his music.

E.C.:
We're becoming automatic. Everybody's getting meaner.

J.S.:
So how do we combat all that?

E.C.:
Not by worrying about your physical fitness.

J.S.:
You're not a big fan of the jogging scene.

E.C.:
Tell me—how'd you get this sickness?

J.S.:
It's an unconscious extension of America's jock culture, I suppose. You're saying there are more important things to worry about.

E.C.:
I see things that I don't fancy.

J.S.:
Like?

96

E.C.:
Everybody's got their orders. You have to do your duty . . . taking
orders from the kingdom.

J.S.:
The scene in England, particularly among the youth, seems a lot
heavier than it is here. The forming of Rock Against Racism is a
good example of that.

E.C.:
Mr. Oswald, with his swastika tattoo . . . There's a vacancy waiting
on the English boob tube. [Oswald Mosley is one of the leaders
of England's National Front.]

J.S.:
As an American it's very hard to fathom such a movement gaining
support.

E.C.:
Face the music, face the facts. There's no such thing as an
original sin.

J.S.:
And?

E.C. [*smugly*]:
Here we are living in Paradise . . . living in luxury.

J.S.:
You consider the situation dangerous.

E.C.:
They bite much worse than their bark. We may never be the
same again.

J.S.:
Maybe we can part on a lighter note. [Costello laughs, hurriedly
writes something in his notebook.] You've had great success of late.

E.C.:
I never thought that it would come to this.

J.S.:
And the money?

E.C.:
Once upon a time I had a little money—government burglars took it.

J.S.:
You mean your finances have not—

E.C.:
Why don't we call it day?

J.S.:
Well, I had a few more questions.

E.C.:
I would have thought you'd have had enough by now.

J.S.:
A last word?

E.C.:
[*closes his notebook, stands, and smiles*]: Forget your fancy manners.
Forget your English grammar.

(Photo: C. Grabowski)

Elvis Costello

Steely Dan

(ABC Records photo)

STEELY DAN

While unabashedly breaking all the rules, Steely Dan remains one of the most popular bands in the world. However, there is no band. Steely Dan is Walter Becker and Donald Fagen. Together they write, compose, participate in, and oversee the creation of each Steely Dan recording. They regularly employ studio musicians, dismissing their peers' contention that it distorts the purity of the music.

Their accessibility to the media is virtually nonexistent; even when they do consent to a very rare interview, they reveal nothing about themselves or their music.

Finally, they do not perform live. There are no Steely Dan concerts to attend, no national tours, no TV or film appearances. Yet they have received multiple accolades, including a few gold and platinum records.

As Donald Fagen was heard to say, "It is kinda strange, isn't it?"

Bruce Springsteen

BRUCE SPRINGSTEEN

GROWING UP

Beyond the Palace hemi-powered drones
scream down the boulevard
The girls comb their hair in rear-view mirrors
And the boys try to look so hard
The amusement park rises bold and stark
Kids are hunched on the beach in a mist
I wanna die with you out on the streets tonight
In an everlasting kiss

    "Born to Run"
    Bruce Springsteen

ASBURY PARK

Early May, and the shore community is already more than a month into the summer's preparations. Each morning, two gigantic bulldozers tear at the rotting wood of the boardwalk, filling dump trucks with the splintered aftermath. A dozen men follow in their wake, replacing the damaged sections with newly cut, smoothly sanded planks. The men wear carpenters' belts and carry hammers, which they use to secure each new piece. The nails they use are tightly clenched in their teeth.

Along the expanse of the boardwalk, concession owners are busy repairing the effects of a cold, bitter winter. Flakes of salt-drenched paint are scraped away, and the booths are repainted. Broken windows are replaced, and where the wind has made holes in a canopy, the canvas is mended.

The amusement rides are tended to; the diesel motors that turn them are tuned and greased. Their large looming metal arms are oiled, and seats and handles are cleaned. New rides arrive in gigantic trucks. Old ones are dismantled and packed into precise piles of steel poles, gears, and cogwheels.

One man is at work checking the bolts that hold the swings of the Ferris wheel in place. He stands on a seat, stretching to tighten a nut. The seat is roughly thirty feet from the ground. An ocean wind lashes at the Ferris wheel, causing the seat to sway. The man seems unaware of any potential peril.

On the south side of town, a block in from the boards, stands the Palace, an indoor amusement center. With the exception of the harshest days of winter, the Palace stays open year round. It is a large rectangular building, laced with flashing, imploring lights and filled with the fantasy sounds of pinball machines and penny-arcade carny wheels. On its exterior, extending from the roof into the sky, is a giant neon clown in blinking red, green, and white. His bugaboo eyes and curling smile advertise the pleasures to be found within.

There is a merry-go-round just as you step inside. As you spin around, you lean far over from your wooden horse and try to grab a protruding ring from a slim metallic device barely within reach. A brass ring entitles you to a free ride.

Farther on are the usual phone booths and penny-ante games of chance, but toward the rear, past the two long rows of pinball machines, is the Tilt-a-Whirl—not just any Tilt-a-Whirl, but Crazy Charlie's Tilt-a-Whirl.

Charlie has been working at the Palace for twenty years. He looks to be well into the final portion of his life and dresses the part of an old carnival barker. He wears a change belt strapped to his slim middle and, invariably, a weird tie-dyed T-shirt and an even weirder feathered hat. He works his ride with cool precision and a touch of pride. Even now, when most rides are run by bored teenagers who simply go through the motions, Charlie loads you in, starts the hooded cars slowly, and then, with demonic glee, accelerates the diesel. The more he is implored to slow the ride down, the faster he guns the engine. If you scream, "Stop!" he's sure to keep you going until your stomach forces its way up into your throat.

Near the tiny booth where he triggers the giant toy and sips at cardboard containers of coffee all day, a half dozen or so young men congregate. Charlie's domain is their hangout, the one place where they feel comfortable and in control. They all wear leather jackets—not the overtly sexual leather of the macho crowd, but the cool, secret leather of midnight marauding dudes, the young Romeos of Asbury, who drink from bottles of sweet wine under the Boardwalk and wear sneakers for sure footing as they sprint through the alleys away from the cops.

They watch the summer's preparatory construction with disdain. To them it represents the all-too-quick return of the multitude of strangers who invade their territory each and every summer. To them Asbury is home, not a vacation spot. And the Boardwalk, the ocean, the cheap bars are all embedded within their lives, as familiar as the worn jeans they slide into each morning. Their language is fraught with private references and nicknames like Wild Billy, Gary G., Spanish Johnny, and the Wolf.

They refer to the summer visitors as outsiders, intruders, and to the daughters they bring with them as city virgins.

Between the long run of the Boardwalk and the city block of motels and hotels is Ocean Avenue. It extends the entire length of the boards and then curls back toward the Palace in a wide arc. The natives call this stretch of road the Circuit. It serves as the starting point, most evenings, for a ritual that has been going on for more than a decade.

Past nine o'clock, when the moon hangs low over the ocean, the Circuit fills with cars. Massive machines, low-lying "wheels" humming with horsepower. The drivers move slowly round and round the Circuit, checking out the occupants of the other cars, hoping to connect for a long, wild night. Cruising continues until, a connection

Springsteen

Springsteen

(Photo: C. Frick)

made, arrangements are settled upon and two cars blast away from the checkout point, heading for a deserted strip of beach or shared drinks in some local bar.

One of the more popular bars, situated in the midst of the ritual's melee, is the Stone Pony. Each evening, particularly during the bloat of summer, scores of people come to the Pony to carouse. The Pony's top performer has always been a skinny kid with grease-black hair who sings in a grating, gravel voice. He is a local guy, a street cat, and the outlaw space that Wild Billy, Spanish Johnny, and the Palace Boys occupy is his space too. He is nicknamed the Boss, but he is known to millions of strangers by his given name: Bruce Springsteen.

Actually, Springsteen grew up in Freehold, a small community up the Parkway a bit from Asbury, but Asbury has always been his haunting ground. He lives it, breathes it, and writes about it. Even now, when he has been deemed a bona-fide superstar, he chooses to live in the Atlantic Highlands outside Asbury. His songs are full of the churning rush, the lunatic fringe of a city that exists for nothing other than pure pleasure and wild abandon.

"My songs reflect the way I grew up," Springsteen once explained. "It was the typical Jersey-shore thing—surfing, cars, pinball. There's been so much written about it now it's like, I don't know, unreal or somethin'. But it's very real to me and my friends. When I was playin' bars all those years there was a place called the Upstage Club. And that was the place where everybody'd go after their gigs to wind down, to work out your own songs and stuff. You'd go there after a gig, play until five, six a.m. if you wanted to, then go home, sleep, maybe cop some sleep on the beach, and start all over again the next night. That was what growin' up was all about.

"I don't know, I never thought about it, but I suppose that kinda thing doesn't go on up [in northern New Jersey] or whatever.

Springsteen at work. Behind him is "the Big Man"—saxophonist Clarence Clemons.

(Photo: C. Frick)

Let's face it—Asbury's an *amusement park*. It's not, like, you know, another city."

It is true that Asbury's unique carnival ambiance has always had a very strong hold on Springsteen; when his parents chose to move to California, Bruce stayed behind. "I'd already had it with school. And the guitar was like the only way I could express myself. I felt comfortable behind it, right? I was playin' a lot of the time, and it just didn't make any sense to me to move away. Besides, me and my dad weren't exactly gettin' along then." He laughs, the kind of inner laugh prompted by the memories of screamin', close-to-blows fights that seem to dominate the childhood of many rebels.

Springsteen's decision not to follow his parents to the coast was, in a way, the turning point of the young man's life. Unlike his compatriots "Southside" Johnny Lyon and "Miami" Steve Van Zandt, Springsteen had never bothered with "dày jobs." ("There really wasn't anything else Bruce could do," a friend remarked.) With his family gone, he was forced into an almost relentless pursuit of fame—a pursuit with which he had always been involved but one that now became an obsession. He was growing older, into his twenties, and a full-time, profitable career in music was becoming possible for him.

He already had a small, loyal following. "Every time Bruce showed up at a club," remembers a musician friend, "people would start yelling for him to take the stage. I think we all knew he was headed for big things."

Springsteen's constituency guaranteed him work—club owners have always had a special affection for kids who can fill their places with ,a crowd. He played the entire length of the Jersey shore, fronting a number of bands, although none ever felt exactly right. "I've always been a solo act," he offers. "Even the E Streeters

(Photo: C. Frick)

Southside

Southside

[his current band, perhaps the best in-concert group working at the moment] aren't *me*. They're the guys playin' my stuff with me."

While remaining active on the shore circuit, Springsteen began to take his solo act (an acoustic guitar and a harmonica, occasionally augmented by a piano) into Manhattan, in particular to the Village's folk clubs.

During one of these trips, Springsteen decided to approach Mike Appel, the founder of Laurel Canyon Productions. (Appel had come to New York from California, where he had known brief fame working with Wes Farrel, of TV's *Partridge Family* fame.)

Springsteen walked into Appel's office, guitar in hand, and played him a tune he had written about two deaf people dancing to a rock 'n' roll band. As Appel recalls, he wasn't especially impressed.

Undaunted, Springsteen returned six months later (he had been in California visiting his parents) with a portfolio of songs, most of which were to become his first album, *Greetings from Asbury Park*. He called Appel from an outdoor phone booth, bugging Appel's secretary until she finally put him through to Mike. Springsteen reminded Appel of their prior meeting and asked if he could play for him again.

"When?" Appel wondered.

"How about right now?" Springsteen answered. "I'm just down the street."

Appel invited him up. Again, Springsteen went into Appel's office and began to play. The song was "Hard to Be a Saint in the City."

When Springsteen came to the line "like a Harley in heat," Appel told him to stop. "I've heard enough," he told the anxious

Springsteen. "I want you on Laurel Canyon." Springsteen signed a contract that very day.

Appel and Springsteen became immediate friends. Bruce was attracted to Appel's bad-boy street brashness (a characteristic the two shared) and cunning business head. Appel entertained Springsteen with stories of the times he'd spent with Buddy Holly and Gene Vincent (two of Bruce's idols), and thus began the most notorious rock partnership since Elvis Presley met Colonel Tom Parker. (Ironically, Springsteen once described the relationship to journalist Dave Marsh in those very terms. Springsteen related, "Mike once told me, 'You be Elvis and I'll be the colonel.' The problem was, I wasn't Elvis, and Mike wasn't the colonel.")

Appel's approach was dynamite charged. He contacted CBS, demanding to see John Hammond, Sr., the man credited with discovering Billie Holiday, Barbra Streisand, and Bob Dylan, among others. He sent word to Hammond that he had an artist who would put the rest of Columbia's roster to shame.

Hammond agreed to audition Springsteen in his office. Springsteen recalls, "Mike and me went to [Hammond's] office. Mike was like . . . you know, confident, pushy. Sorta dominating everything. So we're in this huge office, and Hammond says, 'Why don't you play something?' I was thinkin', *Well, this is it—you either do it here or it's back to the bars, kid.* So I just played. The whole time I'm thinkin', *What are me and Mike doing in this guy's office, anyway?*"

Springsteen left the office with a contract. "When Hammond said, 'We want you to make an album,' I went crazy. That was my dream all those years—to make a record. And at that moment I just went crazy."

The ensuing difficulties between Springsteen and Appel have become rock 'n' roll history. Briefly, somewhere between the release of

The Wild, the Innocent, and the E Street Shuffle and the subsequent release of Born to Run, Springsteen found that his contract was not only ironbound but also stifling. Although neither party has made known full details of the contract, it is generally believed that Springsteen had signed away nearly everything but his right to breathe.

The situation led to suits and countersuits and was eventually settled out of court for an undisclosed amount of money (Springsteen paying Appel to "leave" Laurel Canyon). However, the litigation was not without its troubles. During the legal battles, Springsteen was issued a court order forbidding him to record or perform while the issue was pending. Neither Springsteen nor Appel could forsee that the issue would take *three years* to settle.

Springsteen told *Rolling Stone's* Dave Marsh, "The litigation was all very distressing to me. It was all a loss of control. It had a bad effect on my control of myself. Which is why I initially started playing, and why I play. That's what upset me the most about it. I was very, very naïve. It was like being in a car with somebody who had the gas pedal pushed to the floor . . . and you can't do anything about stopping him!"

It is fortunate, and a sign of strength on his behalf, that Springsteen's talents were not destroyed by the problem. If anything, his poetic skills were sharpened. His vision became more clear; he was forced into maturity.

His first album, *Greetings from Asbury Park,* made during the "good times" between Bruce and Appel, is a solid piece of work, a kind of *Portrait of the Artist as a Teenager Coming of Age in Asbury Park.* All the Palace characters are there—Crazy Janey, the Mission Man, Wild Young Billy, and G-Man. Springsteen expounds on their nightly pattern—how they dress sharp, cruise the Circuit, and then head up to Greasy Lake (actually a swamp in the nether lands off Route 9) for a party.

There is the ragamuffin drummer, home from the army, who feels lost and alienated. The girls on the boardwalk scorn him. He spends his time racing his superstock at the drags. So fast, so furious, he smacks into a brick wall and buries himself beneath his smoking metal. Throughout *Greetings,* Springsteen reminds us that adolescence was a constant struggle with teachers, parents, and the entire adult world. School was hanging out with one leg bent against the brick wall and a cigarette poked into the corner of your mouth. Breaking the rules was the only true way to maintain your independence.

Next came *The Wild, the Innocent, and the E Street Shuffle* (released in 1973, produced by Mike Appel). Springsteen plunged deeper, this time adding the nightlife of Manhattan and the outlaw environs of Spanish Harlem and the Lower East Side to his poetry. Puerto Rican Jane and Spanish Johnny play out a futuristic *West Side Story* scenario. "New York City Serenade" celebrates the thousand and one mysteries that lie ahead after dusk on any given day in the city. There is a beautiful song about a girl returning to the shore after an affair with a "city dude." In a sad confession ("Fourth of July, Asbury Park [Sandy]"), Springsteen laments that the frivolity of the boardwalk is growing old and stale. It may be time to move on. Yet the lament is rhetorical, as if Bruce is convinced that no matter what may arise, he will stay.

Born to Run, Springsteen's third album, was the monster Appel had waited for. It was the record responsible for Springsteen's national recognition. Emulating Phil Spector's patented "wall of sound," the album literally blasted its way into the public's consciousness.

Suddenly, Springsteen's name was on everyone's lips. Multiple major press notices followed, including the covers of both *Time* and *Newsweek.* Springsteen had arrived.

119

The twist of fate was that his relationship with Appel was on the verge of collapse. Rock critic Jon Landau (who had met Bruce shortly after he had published an overwhelming column praising Springsteen and calling him the future of rock 'n' roll) filled Appel's shoes. He became Springsteen's confidant and overseer, leaving his post at *Rolling Stone* in order to have more time (and a freer rein) with which to aid and abet his comrade.

Born to Run was not so much cynical as it was penetrating. Again it was evident that the difficulties with Laurel Canyon coupled with his rapidly growing success had left their mark on Bruce. Asbury Park was changing or, better, with each album Springsteen was unwittingly revealing his secret world to a nation of strangers. That world sounded so attractive on vinyl that droves of young fans were heading to the Jersey shore in hopes of capturing the magic of which he sang. In "Night," he wrote:

You get up every morning at the sound of the bell
You get to work late and the boss man's givin' you hell
Till you're out on a midnight run

Losing your heart to a beautiful one
And it feels right
As you lock up the house
Turn out the lights
And step out into the night

And the world is bustin' at its seams
And you're just a prisoner of your dreams
Holding on for your life
'Cause you work all day
To blow 'em away in the night

as if to say that together we can *still* escape the parents and adults—this time expanding the adult world to include managers, businessmen, and record-company executives.

"Backstreets" is one long last sigh dedicated to Bruce's easy days of playing for fun instead of for keeps. At that time there was also a song called "The Promise" that Bruce hadn't recorded but was playing in concert. He performed it alone at the piano. It was his very personal goodbye to Appel. It emphasized the naïveté of both of them but heartbreakingly returned to a refrain that wailed, "In the end the promise was broken."

With the triumph of *Born to Run*, Springsteen became a star, his live shows legendary for their intensity and expertise. He was stuck within the apex of his troubles with Appel while at the same time struggling with all the particulars that come with super-success. (No matter how prepared one feels he or she may be for major stardom, once those heights are reached the various pressures, the loss of privacy, the relentless demands on time, etc., all come as sharp, unexpected blows.)

Springsteen chose *Darkness on the Edge of Town,* his fourth album, as the vehicle with which he would come to grips with his past and affirm his future. A fully matured, riveting work, *Darkness* served as both his exorcism and his baptism. If *Greetings* was his *Portrait of the Artist as a Young Man, Darkness* was *You Can't Go Home Again* without the unresolvable resentment of Wolfe but certainly with the same melancholy conclusion—home will never be the same; much has changed. As Springsteen once mused, "After I signed with Columbia, after that one moment of like goin' crazy, then began a new reality."

Darkness includes all of Springsteen's familiar characters—the Brando-emulating punks, the lost-in-the-flood heroes, the mixed-up, fiercely independent woman—but they've all grown. It's hard enough to be a rebellious late-night teen, Springsteen seems to be saying, but it's even more difficult to be a young adult *still* searching

121

for the promised land.

There is desperation on this album. Springsteen writes: "You're born with nothin' and better off that way. Soon as you got something, they send somebody to try and take it away." He continues: "Baby, I got my facts learned real good right now—poor man wanna be rich, rich man wanna be king, and the king ain't satisfied until he's got everything." In "Promised Land" he screams: "Sometimes I feel so weak I just want to explode. Explode and tear this whole town apart. Take a knife and cut this pain from my heart."

But Springsteen also tells us that his anger and frustration have been properly lanced—the therapeutic value of writing about them has left him cleansed. Springsteen rejects the notion that *Darkness* is a desperate statement. He admits there is some despondency but prefers to emphasize the aftereffects of his exorcism. "Badlands" has him defiantly stating: "Honey I want the heart, I want the soul, I want control right now." As if to warn unscrupulous "business types" who may attempt to corral him into a too-binding contract or want more of him than he's willing to give, he silently but authoritatively affirms: "I live now only with strangers. I talk to only strangers. I walk with Angels that have no place. So don't go looking in my face."

With *Darkness* behind him and his legal battles won, Springsteen is free to do the one and only thing that ever really mattered to him—write and play music to the best of his ability. He has said that his next album will consist of "more early-English kind of things. Ya know, not quite so intense. There'll be a lot of fun on the album."

He also seems to genuinely enjoy his success once again. He has been through his trial by fire and emerged singed but not badly burned. The best example I saw of this occurred backstage in an offhand comment to a journalist. The journalist had cornered

Springsteen and made the oft-repeated request that Bruce comment
on his dealings with Appel. With no malice and little effort,
Springsteen smiled and said: "I really don't have anything to say.
I just came here to play some music."

In concert during the 1979 tour.

SPRINGSTEEN LIVE !

Man, can that cat play!
  —Chuck Berry

One of the greatest live shows I've seen in a real long time.
  —Jackson Browne

*I've never known him to play anything less than all out. He's
probably one of the few guys I know who's never slouched onstage,
never gave less than 100 percent.*
  —Southside Johnny

If there is one matter upon which there is total accord in the rock
world, it is the perfection that Springsteen exhibits in concert.
The intensity of his performances is almost unparalleled. He gives his
all to his audience, most times striving for even more. As he explains:
"Playing keeps me honest. Each time I go out there I'm reminded
of what it's all about. . . . I'm able to make records, to make a
living playing music because of the people out there. So I give
everything I got. Every time. I wouldn't feel right if I didn't."

I've seen Springsteen at work on numerous occasions, but two
evenings stand out as special. The first was his debut performance
in August 1975 at Manhattan's Bottom Line. The second was a
weekend gig at the inception of his 1978 tour, a tour that marked
the end of his three-year moratorium on performing.

OPENING NIGHT, THE BOTTOM LINE, AUGUST 1975

A single spotlight shone on a piano as Springsteen came on stage
alone. His hair, winding around his head in tight curls, was covered
by a poor boy cap he wore flopped to one side. He was wearing
sneakers (black Cons) and bleached denims. Over his T-shirt hung
a rich black leather jacket. He began with a soft melody, a song
about changing and growing. As the tune ended, he jumped up,
stage lights blazing, and the E Street Band took the stage.
Clarence Clemons, a hefty black guy, premier saxophonist, wore a

virgin white suit complete with white patent-leather shoes. Steve
Van Zandt, lead guitarist, complemented Clemons's outfit with his
own sparkling red one.

They launched into "Tenth Avenue Freeze Out," ice-cold funk,
playing with both power and passion. Springsteen stood stage
center, legs spread wide, shoulders hunched, his leather wrapped
tight around his torso. He spun, twirled, gyrating back and forth with
a great show of energy while growling out the songs. He doesn't
so much sing as he uses his gravel voice to punctuate the poetry
of his lyrics as he croaks them out. He'll screach a wild soul yelp
and then suddenly drop to a whisper, the band so tight they
seem to be a part of him—pausing when he does and lashing out
with adrenaline abandon when he signals them for emphasis.
He crouched near the audience, feeding on their response, bobbing
his head up and down, teasing with the collar of his jacket. He
looked like a Spanish pirate; his skin was tanned dark; puffs of
hair bearded his face. One ear was adorned with a gold earring.

He did "Spirit in the Night" early in the set, changing the accent
of the music so that it became more of a short story than a song.

All the time alive with motion, "giving skin" to Clemons, pirouetting
across the stage with the mike tightly clutched in one hand. The
music was blaring, the sax blasting away while piggybacking a
guitar lead. Then WHAM!—it fell to a sweet melody while Springsteen broke into a spontaneous monologue.

He would emulate the rhythmic speech of city youth, floating it
in and out of his songs. The band performed with brilliance, belting
out long, flowing rolls of music or tenderly lacing about
Springsteen's lyrics.

Springsteen strapped on his Fender for a rendition of the old
Searchers' song "Every Time You Walk in the Room." He kept the

guitar on, playing fiercely, wielding it like a tire iron. He totally captivated his audience, taking them with him through his secret world of cool Romeos and romantic Juliets.

Strutting like a proud rooster, he worked his way through extended, punching jams, squeezing sweat and bated-breath excitement out of the audience. By the time the band launched into "Rosalita," a furious runaway love song, the entire Bottom Line was swaying in syncopated frenzy, on their feet and cheering intensely.

For an encore Springsteen was the late-night drunken wildcat, skipping along the boardwalk as the ocean breeze drenched his swollen wine-red face. He did Gary U.S. Bond's classic "Quarter to Three," whipping around the stage, doing splits, working the music into a fever pitch. He finally dived onto Federici's organ, gyrating like Presley let loose, a wide smile on his face. In one last explosion, the band burst into the final chords and were off-stage, leaving the audience on its feet screaming in post-orgasmic delight.

As people left the club, they spoke incessantly of the show; the magnitude, the strength, and the talent they'd just witnessed. Many were in awe, knocked out by the street angel who had just poured out his life for them.

Springsteen was that good.

A FURIOUS SOUND—SUMMER 1978 TOUR

With all the fury of true rock 'n' roll in their veins, Bruce Springsteen and the E Street Band took to the road for an extensive tour and came away, once again, as the top purveyors of rock 'n' roll since the Stones' first American tour more than a decade ago.

Springsteen was in top form. His manner was lean, cut to the bone. There were no frills; just straight-on heavy midsection jabbing, until each evening the crowd was on its feet cheering the champ on to the crown. The E Street Band was equally devastating, following Bruce's every move as if they were connected to him. They were a relentless bunch, backing up their boss with a solid wall of music.

At each hall, a fifteen-foot extension had been added to the stage, allowing Springsteen ample room to frolic. And Bruce and Clemons did just that—vamping the audience into frenzy upon frenzy. Bittan and Federici's keyboards perfectly complemented the guitar work of Bruce, Miami Steve, and Tallent. Clemons's sax work was powerful enough to split atoms. Mighty Max Weinberg's drums were so strong it felt as if his bass pedal were connected to the inner workings of the earth.

If a ten-minute standing ovation at the finish of each concert was any indication, the band's weekend stopover at Philadelphia's Spectrum left more than forty thousand persons convinced they had witnessed some of the best rock 'n' roll ever performed.

Both concerts began later than had been announced, allowing the audience to settle in their seats while anticipation boiled within them until, when the houselights were dimmed, they exploded with a roar as earsplitting as that of a rocket at takeoff. The band came out umbrella'd by a ceiling of blue and red spotlights.

Bruce, dressed to kill in a black three-piece suit and satin ruby shirt, strapped on his Fender, and the band burst into "Badlands." It was immediately obvious that above all else, Springsteen has been working on his guitar licks over the past few years. His instrument literally sang, and his lead work was impeccable. That is not to say that Van Zandt seemed in anyway concerned—in fact, Springsteen's burning leads seem to stimulate Van Zandt into his own infrared licks. The two flashed blasts of electric steel to and fro much like hotshot surfers sharing a wave.

The evenings were not without surprises, a major one being Springsteen's choice of material. At one time Springsteen had remarked, much to the chagrin of his fans, that he felt the songs on his first album were too long and drawn out and that he probably wouldn't be performing them in concert any more. Of late, someone—one likes to think it was Patti Smith or Robert Gordon or maybe even John Hammond, Sr.—must have persuaded him otherwise. Someone must have reassured him of the simple truth that his earlier tunes are incredible poetic works, for Springsteen performed almost all of his first album. "For You" was done early in the evening, the cogency of it knocking everyone, the multitude of press included, for a loop. There was Springsteen, guitar hip-low, rasping out the story of a contemporary love affair gone sour. The song was done a bit faster this time around, but it wasn't so much the speed of it as the absolute vehemence of the delivery that was stunning. It was as if Springsteen had rediscovered the song. He all but screamed out the final verses, bringing Roy Bittan's high-register ivory tickling with him, modulating the E Streeters until they split wide open into a waterfall of sound.

"Spirit in the Night" was a perfect platform for an aborted attempt at rock 'n' roll theater. After a searing sax break by Clemons, the band ground to a halt midway into "Spirits" and Springsteen disappeared. Suddenly, four tiers above the stage—some two hundred feet away from the band—a lone spotlight was directed into an entrance ramp. Suddenly Springsteen ran through the archway into the aisles, cordless mike in hand. The audience responded by mobbing Bruce, forcing a half retreat to the first tier and a soulful rendering of "Me and Janey Makin' Love in the Dirt" while three female pubescents tried to split Springsteen up evenly into a carry-home order.

A crackling wail, and Bruce dived back on stage, and the band, without missing a beat, crescendoed to a brutal finale. Breathless, Springsteen rasped, "I hope nobody got hurt up there." He was

130

assured that the only damage done was the momentarily increased heartbeats of a dozen or so females who had been close enough to their idol to grab at his body.

"Growing Up" and "Hard to Be a Saint in the City" were done back to back. Springsteen shouted, "When they said sit down, I said *shut up!*" and thousands of teenagers screamed the refrain of defiance.

With his new material, he staggered the audience. On "Prove It All Night," he worked closely with Clemons, both of them literally hopping about with exuberance. "The Big Man," as Bruce called Clemons, was radiant in what Springsteen described as "his fifteenth or sixteenth white suit." Clemons was blowing up a storm as he and Bruce took to the stage's extension, mimicking each other's dance steps, urging the audience on to tornado-like fury. Bruce would stand on one side of the extension, his guitar poking from between his legs, hesitate, then bound across the floor. Clemons would respond with a fanatical jumping jack. Around them, the remainder of the band demonstrated their enthusiasm with a virtual tantrum of sound.

"Racin' in the Streets," the lament of a dragster who's come to see the waning days of souped-up cars and drag racing, slowed the band to a pace that allowed Springsteen full use of his voice. The unmistakable inflections, the gritty, raw-edged moans and howls, were all there. When Springsteen took out a mouth harp and proceeded to play a solo, the entire house fell into silence.

Harmonica still in hand, Springsteen followed "Racin' " with "Thunder Road." A quiet background, cathedral-like, took "Thunder Road" into "Jungleland." Springsteen went to his knees, calling forth the sweat, the womb of night, and the inherent violence of street life. At the finish—down to an almost prone position on stage—he opened wide his lungs, crying out desperation and

131

(Photo: P. Ceccola)

Babe Ruth

wne backstage with close friend David Lindley (left) and Bruce Springsteen (center).

demanding pity.

A quick count, "One, two, three," and the band ripped into
"Adam Raised a Cain." In what must be interpreted as shades of the
radical sixties, the entire band raised their hands in a double-fisted
power salute as Springsteen roared the chorus. With his cohorts
in full power, Bruce squeezed a lead out of his Fender so hot that
it must have sent a good deal of Philly's canine population into
agony. Not to be outdone, Van Zandt cut back with a blast of
his own. The two faced each other, and a duel ensued. Springsteen
attacked his strings. Van Zandt went into a frontal assult. The
fever got so high that Clemons, in mock concern, came between
both of them, begging them to cease. Of course, this only prompted
them into a ferocious jam.

The weekend—and the following months of concerts—belonged to
Springsteen. Nowhere was that more evident than in the final
moments of each show. He did a cover of the Stones' "Mona,"
into "Mickey's Monkey," into his own "She's the One."

In the aftermath of this medley (a consistent hum of approval
arising from the audience), Springsteen paused, laughed aloud, and
shouted into the mike: "This is for you, Rosie—wherever you are!"
"Rosalita (Come Out Tonight)" was done as exquisitely as
Chateaubriand at the Plaza.

After his three-year absence from the scene, the pressure was on
Springsteen. Like a champ, he chose to take that pressure and use it
to his best advantage. His absence could have left him paunchy
and punch drunk. Instead, he returned ready for a fight. It was no
surprise that each night ended in a clean knockout.

134

Bruce and the E Street Band at their New York debut. Left to right: Clemons, Bruce, Weinberg on drums, and Miami Steve Van Zandt. Bassist Garry Tallent is hidden behind Miami.

(Photo: C. Frick)

(Photo: C. DeAlmeida)

Patti Smith: "If I'd known there was gonna be so many of you here, I would have washed my hair!"

Patti Smith before her first standing-room-only audience.

(Photo: C. DeAlmeida)

Patti Smith

(Arista Records photo)

Lou Reed

Lou Reed: "I really can't talk to you about Lou Reed. I don't really know him at all."

Reed is probably rock's most intelligent practitioner. In the mid-seventies he was awarded the literary world's prestigious CCLM Award for a poem he published in the Paris Review. This is not to discount his posturing as the absolutely wild man of the scene, in person and in concert. He constantly appears as if he is about to plunge head-first into the dangerous side of his psyche. His characters move within a world that Poe or Berryman would comprehend better than his contemporaries. Reed's "Heroin" is a classic, as are "Sweet Jane" and "Walk on the Wild Side."

Lou Reed

(Photo: C. Frick)

THE ROAD WAY

Bert Holman, Associate Director of Management Activities, Monarch Entertainment:

"A group decides to go out on tour for one of two reasons—either to make money or to promote a newly released album. If they're going out on promotion, the economics are not so overwhelming. The record company offers tour support, which means simply that they will cover any deficit that may remain if the gross income from the ticket sales does not cover all the projected expenses. The band attempts to stay within its projected budget; yet, unlike the concern that develops when a group is out on tour simply to make money, there isn't the concern that if the ticket sales are disappointing or expenses run over, the group will be losing money. Of course, no band goes out on a major tour—whether it's for promotion or to earn some cash—before the record company's accountants and the band's people have sat down, gone over the figures, and, as best as is possible using projections, both come to the conclusion that the tour will either make money or break even.

"If a band goes out on tour to make money, if there's no new album they are pushing, the tour arrangements become very precise, particularly the financial end. I'll meet with the band's accountants, and we'll work to set up a budget where all of the band's personal needs [transportation, food, laundry, pocket money] are met for the duration of the tour, and after expenses, they still go home with money in their pockets. The more money they want to make, the more they are willing to cut down on luxuries. They'll double up hotel rooms, for instance. Cut down on the use of limousines from the concert hall to the hotel. Where possible, they'll opt for automobile traveling instead of airplanes [usually if the gigs are within four to six hundred miles of each other], cut their stage crew down to the bare minimum—things of that nature.

"Tour expenses include sound-equipment rentals, lighting-equipment rentals, commissions to agencies that book the shows, commissions to managers, air transport, hotels, buses for the band, buses for the crew, per diem for band and crew, payroll and payroll taxes, insurance on the equipment, liability insurance, new equipment for the tour, repairs on equipment throughout the tour, supplies [including tubes, fuses, guitar strings, piano tuner, stage directions, etc.] and, in some cases, attorney's fees [if a group is touring out of the country, an attorney must be hired to deal with the immigration matters].

"A major act goes out on the road with an entourage of approximately thirty people, including the band. An average tour lasts anywhere from 45 to 120 days. You try to squeeze in as many performing nights as possible. If a band can go seven nights straight, that's a tour that's going to make money. Each night you don't play constitutes an entire day off, and the tour ends up losing money that day since the band's still paying out expenses without earning any money on that day. The accountants, *anyone* involved with the money end of the deal, dread a day off—it can set the final gross receipts into a spin. That's why the logistics of a tour are so important. You try to set it up so that there is a gig waiting for the band at every stop along the way. Ideally, it should be a sold-out stop, but that's not always the case. You have to figure that a tour is going to cost you anywhere from six to ten thousand dollars a day to operate. We're talking about expenses of five hundred thousand dollars or up by the time the tour is finished.

"My job basically comes down to figuring out the logistics, pulling together all the disparate functions so that the tour runs successfully. Before I meet with the band, they've already compiled a list of the places across the country where they are booked. When I meet with the band, the first thing we do is go over the itinerary, and then I contact a travel agent. We'll need plane transportation from major city to major city, buses and equipment trucks for the haul between the major stops, and limousines. That involves a rental agency. So then the travel agent, the rental-agency people, and myself plot things out so that there will be hotel accommodations and vehicles waiting for the entourage at every stop along the way.

"Okay, now how do you pay for all these things? Most hotels and rental agencies won't bill any more—they want cash or credit cards. The band's reluctant to put out cash, particularly at the start of the tour when there's no inflowing cash, so the best answer is to put all the expenses on plastic. Unfortunately, a lot of rock people can't get credit cards! One of the first things an accountant encourages his client to do is establish credit, but most of the rockers have been scuffling for so many years that their credit rating isn't exactly A plus. If he or she doesn't have plastic, then it's up to the group's backers—be it the record company or their own production company—to 'donate' the use of their credit cards until the finish of the tour.

"Considerations for the rooms are that they must be close enough to the concert halls to be convenient—a lot of bands like to return to their rooms between the sound check and that evening's performance—and, if not luxurious, at least clean and comfortable. The rented vehicles must be specifically outfitted to haul sound equipment.

"A responsible lighting and sound company must be hired for each gig; that's my responsibility also. The promoters of each hall or arena must be contacted so that the equipment crew is accommodated correctly. When they arrive at 11:00 a.m. to set up for that evening's performance the doors should be open, and there should be provisions for breakfast, lunch, and dinner for the crew. Showers should be available in the event that the crew won't have the time to return to their hotel rooms before the gig. Basically, as far as the crew's concerned, you try to cut down on the amount of time they have to spend on their personal lives—that's food, laundry, and the like—so that they can do their jobs correctly without concerning themselves with the amenities that make life on the road less of a hassle.

"The band collects the money for each performance *before* they go onstage that night, in theory anyway. The usual breakdown is 15 percent to the promoter, 85 percent to the band—after hall expenses. In a smaller hall like New York's Palladium [seating thiry-five hundred], the figures came to, say, $8,500 for the band, $1,500 for the promoter. In a place like the Garden, a band might gross $160,000, which means they would go home with about $60,000. Not bad for a night's work."

143

(Photo: K. Stechow)

WNEW-FM's Vin Scelsa.

They're trying to anesthetize the way that you feel
—Elvis Costello
"Radio, Radio"

There are several hundred radio stations in the United States working within a rock format. Approximately three-quarters are on AM frequencies, and the rest are on the FM band.

The rock stations air the most popular music (hence "pop rock") in the nation. AM's format is tightly disciplined and relies heavily on a playlist. (A playlist is a compilation of songs that constitute the station's total musical output. It is determined by the station's program director, who in turn draws the list from the industry's weekly charts. The charts, prime indicators of the top-selling artists nationwide, are released weekly by *Billboard, Record World,* and *Cashbox* magazines. The magazines gather their information on record sales by conducting complicated phone surveys of record stores throughout the nation.)

The AM format leaves little if any leeway for the disc jockey (DJ or jock). He or she is more or less an interchangeable part— no more than an overbearing, blaring voice screaming out the time, the weather, and advertisements. There is no place in AM for creativity. It has been swept away, its place taken by the more reliable (and highly sanitized) machine-like method involving the playlist.

FM radio, on the other hand, has always meant creativity, unpredictability, and spontaneity. Whereas AM plays primarily singles (45s), FM is more concerned with cuts from albums. Traditionally, FM has had very little to do with playlists; if one is utilized its use is *suggested*, rather than demanded by management. And the DJ is the predominant force behind the programming. Never more important than the music they play, nonetheless FM jocks *commune* with their audiences. The music they play is carefully selected to blend with their particular attitudes. Listening to a good FM jock

(Photo: K. Stechow)

Scelsa and Saporita.

is somewhat like reading a good book—there are characters, plots, subplots, and the rest, all interwoven by the jock's "rap" and the music she or he plays.

But severe warning signs have risen of late, indicating that the uniqueness of FM may soon be gone. It, too, may become homogenized and tightly structured, and worst of all, it may lose all its identity. There is evidence of this occurring already; although most FM stations still play albums as opposed to singles, more and more often, the same albums are dominating the airways. A number of FM jocks have begun to take on the monotone usually associated with their AM counterparts. A bastardized form of the playlist has been introduced by Lee Abrams, who developed a concept called Superstars. Superstars is a tape comprised of cuts culled from the top-selling albums in the nation. A station subscribes to Abrams's service and each week receives a tape containing the favorite artists of the week (determined by record sales). All a DJ need do is slip the tape on and relax. Between cuts he or she can read the time, weather, and ads.

The portent is frightening. Many of FM's old-timers (the DJs who came into the format at its inception) are both frightened and furious: frightened because they know that should Abrams's methods improve ratings, the DJs will be forced to conform or be out of a job; furious because they fervently believe in what they are doing and they forsee the end of a format that was originally begun (in the late sixties) as a direct protest against the mesmerizing mentality of AM.

One of FM's most notable elders is New York's Vin Scelsa. Scelsa epitomizes the pre-Abrams FM disc jockey. He is an unabashed intellectual, his home virtually awash with books.

Scelsa is a large, rotund man, with an on-again, off-again beard. His "on the air" sound could best be described as a kind of soothing

148

professorial manner of speech frequently punctuated by a deep, infectious chortle. He is at once unpretentious and intelligent. He is acutely aware of the needs and desires of his audience. It is not unusual for his show to include a book review or an off-the-cuff critique of a current theater production. (He is a voracious reader and a well-informed individual. His comments contain all the knowledge and background of an English-lit major.)

He speaks not so much to his listeners as with them; it is as if they are all drawn together by a common bond, consisting of similar musical tastes and similar philosophies.

Puffing on an everpresent briar pipe and adjusting his round-framed glasses, Scelsa comments: "For me, radio has always been a vehicle with which I could express my creativity. I am not a writer, nor am I a painter or a musician. But I feel I am an artist; I have a need to create. And when I started with FM [about 1969 with a New Jersey–based college station], I stumbled onto an area where I could explore my creativity via the music I played and the people who related to what I was playing and saying."

In the decade-plus since Scelsa's first job, he has watched with dismay as the "free form" format of FM has slowly been swept aside to make way for the bleak future—a future where everything revolves around money, where the station's major concern is to garner huge advertising accounts. And accounts are best secured by implementing methods similar to those employed by the AM people: a very tight format; an absolute playlist; and a DJ who lacks any uniqueness or individuality, the antithesis of Scelsa and the handful of other "old-time" FM jocks throughout the nation.

Scelsa recalls: "In the late sixties, when most of us were just starting on college radio, there was a spontaneity, a freedom, a carefreeness that led to experimentation. That was what 'free form' was all about; that was its *raison d'être*. The listener knew that

149

the DJ was the same as he or she was. The jock was discovering
the music at the same time the listener was. The music we were
all listening to, jocks and the audience alike, was reflecting the
changes we were all going through both politically and socially.
In a way, the music was responsible for creating some of those
changes. Certainly, it was aiding in raising people's consciousness.
So each show was a message.

"There was an overall quality that the jocks tried for, a purpose,
if you will. And the purpose was that we wanted the listener to get
something from each program, we wanted to promulgate the
message. And the response was enormous. The audience responded
to what we were doing—combining politics and music. We all
[DJs and audience] took it for granted that we had the same
lifestyle, the same beliefs, the same desires.

"But this was college radio, and we didn't have to worry about
ratings or revenue. Now, when we realized that we could do the
same thing publicly [NBC and ABC implemented FM stations in 1970,
urging Scelsa and his ilk into the industry as professionals], almost
immediately we were reminded that this was a business and
immediately we had to learn to balance business and real com-
munication. So it really has been a struggle since the beginning."

I asked Scelsa, "Although there was a struggle, it did seem that
free form managed to survive. Now, as the eighties approach,
do you fear that the death of free form is at hand?"

"Exactly. You see, it worked like this: as the seventies went on and
the record industry grew from subculture into mass culture, radio got
sucked in to the dream of big bucks. And as the industry grew
larger and larger—into the billion-dollar range—the audience
became more diffused. You could no longer assume that the music
we shared reflected a lifestyle or represented any kind of a common
bond, for that matter. So the executives decided that it was
necessary to go to the tried-and-true formula of appealing to the
lowest common denominator. So you had MOR [middle of the road—
read "dentist's office"] music, you had top forty and soul music
on AM, and suddenly along came AOR—album-oriented radio—

using the same concepts of AM, only adjusting them to the particulars of FM, that is, an audience that listened primarily to albums. And the next step was to institute a program director [for the most part, the DJ had always programmed his or her own music on FM], and then came a playlist.''

"It follows,'' I said, "that Abrams and Superstars wasn't too far behind.''

"That's right. Radio became *primarily* the publicity arm of the music business. Radio promotes the record. So they took the AOR format, packaged it, and sold it around the country, so that by now any city which had a station that had a unique sound or personality suddenly was utilizing this format which frowned upon individuality.

"By now, you could go to virtually any city in the United States and tune in on its number-one FM station, and it would sound exactly like the station in your hometown. It's become universally a mediocre thing. Where you once had a unique sound to a certain community, that's all gone now. It's all neatly packaged, all determined for the DJ before he even steps into the studio.''

"It sounds as if you're saying: (1) Free-form, progressive radio is dead and (2) it is being replaced by a format not unlike AM—a format that forbids creativity.''

"I know, and it's a frightening concept. The DJ is becoming an interchangeable part. See, in the beginning we had a moral commitment—at least most of us did. Now it's just a guy who has a modicum of talent and decides he'd rather play records all day than pump gas. That's your new FM DJ. He *wants* a program director, he *wants* to be told what to do. It's too much work otherwise.''

"So what happens to the Vin Scelsas of the business?''

"Let's just say this—if you rally against them they have only one thing to tell you: 'Fuck off; we don't need you any more.' ''

Benson

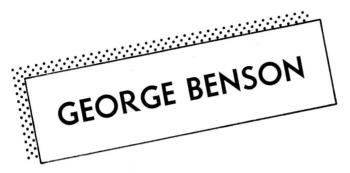

GEORGE BENSON

George Benson is resplendent in a three-piece deep green velvet
suit; the hue of the fabric a perfect complement to the verdant foliage
of his suburban home. A sleek Mercedes is at rest in the driveway.
Within the house is a fully equipped recording studio as well as
a small cinema where once was a den. The furnishings are a study
in tasteful opulence.

Benson owns another house in Hawaii, and he, his wife, and
his two sons divide their time between the two residences.

Benson offers no apologies for his grand style. At age thirty-seven,
with twenty-eight years in the business and some twenty albums
behind him, he feels his recent success is well earned.

Not until the 1976 release of *Breezin'* did fame and fortune find
Benson. *Breezin'* went double platinum and garnered him three
Grammys, one for Best Pop Instrumental, one for the single "This
Masquerade" as Record of the Year, and one for Best Jazz Album.
In Flight and *Weekend in L.A.*, the next two albums, both went
platinum, and *Living Inside Your Love* went double platinum. At
last Benson settled into the comfortable niche of an accomplished
career.

His triumph has not come without criticism, however, particularly
from those jazz purists who feel that Benson, long the "unblemished"
jazz guitarist, sacrificed his creativity for commercialism. He has
been accused of selling out, of purposefully pursuing the big buck.
These accusations come from people who sat back and watched
pop and rock guitarists make millions upon millions, after learning
their licks from Benson. And all the while these accusers extolled
the talents of some "unknown, obscure jazz guitarist" named
George Benson.

There is no anger in Benson's voice when he is called upon to
discuss this situation. His was a conscious decision that, in his mind,

had nothing to do with selling out. It was a decision based, finally, on the reality of his situation.

"You see," he begins in a soft but earnest voice, "I'd hear certain people, men who had become very big stars and very very rich, say that they learned to play guitar by listening to me. And I couldn't understand it. I said to myself, 'How could they be rich and I'm still scuffling for a living?' I knew there was a problem. And I had had it with scuffling. It started to bug me. How could somebody be taking my music and be making it while I was, you know, always just on the outskirts of success?

"You see, I don't think people understand what it's like to play to walls for years. For people to call you the best there is—keep calling you number one, the best jazz guitarist in the world or what have you—and yet nobody *knows* you! You play in a club and you're playing to five people! It becomes a little ridiculous after a while. That's what it's like playing to walls, man. It's frustrating and it hurts .And I don't think people understand it. The people who say, 'Benson went commercial,' or something like that. It wasn't going commercial, what I did. It was just practical. *I didn't want to play to walls for the rest of my life.*

"So what I did was, well, I made a decision on *Breezin'* to go back to singing. I mean, up until then I was known primarily as a guitarist—a lot of cats didn't even know I could sing! Which was ironical 'cause when I was a kid in Pittsburgh playin' in a dozen different bands, that's about all I *did* was sing. I played guitar, if you want to call it that. I'd heard Charlie Christian [the premier jazz axeman] when I was a kid; he was the man responsible for me picking up the guitar in the first place. But as a kid I was playing a kinda funky thing. It wasn't until I got turned on to Charlie Parker that I realized how little I knew about the language of my instrument. So I told myself I was gonna have to stop with this funky stuff and learn to *play* my guitar."

154

Ten-year-old Benson with his first manager.

George Benson

Benson burrowed his way into the underground of jazz, leaving behind his Pittsburgh following and digging on the heels of guys like Wes Montgomery, Kenny Burrell, and Grant Green. His instrumental ability increased tenfold, and he became well-known in the jazz field. In 1967, Benson signed with A and M, then CTI. He released a host of albums, none of which went anywhere beyond the narrow jazz field. His vocal talents were completely ignored.

"As a matter of fact," Benson continues, "I recall *exactly* the moment I realized I had made the right decision in returning to vocals. I had just finished *Breezin'* and was invited to play some of the cuts on WRVR [New York City's top jazz station]. *Breezin'* hadn't been released yet, right? So I asked the DJ to put on 'This Masquerade' [the sweet love song in which Benson's voice is predominant]. All of a sudden the phones at the station lit up like a Christmas tree! That's when I knew I'd made the right decision. Again, it was just practical.

"Look, I'll tell you something that I've learned. I don't care how good you are on your instrument—some people just don't care about instrumentals. They don't *hear* them. But the power of vocals, well, that's a different story, because you're speaking in a language that everyone understands—you're speaking in their tongue. They don't understand the language of guitar or piano or what have you. But people can understand straight words. They understand it when I sing, 'Everything must change.' They know what that means. They say, 'Yeah, hey, I dig that. I know what that cat means.' I feel that the reinstatement, if you will, of vocals is responsible for the upsurge of success in my career. There's no question about it.

"Somethin' else a lot of the folks who criticize me don't realize, and that is because I went quote unquote commercial, I can now afford to do what I want to do musically. In other words, the public is gonna listen more to the language of my guitar because they've understood me through my vocals. I tell young cats now that if they want to make it they've got to play a little bit simpler for the folks, at least until the folks get to know them. You want to be hip? I ask them. Be as hip as you want in your basement or whatever but for the folks if you play just a little bit simpler at first, then you can shake them up later without leaving them behind."

Basking in the comfort of Benson's home, a friend wonders aloud if the compromise was worth it.

"I wouldn't use the word *compromise*," Benson corrects him. "It's more *comprehension*. *Understanding* your audience. But look, I'm here because this is where I always wanted to be. I worked very very hard and long for it. I'm not about to apologize to anyone for it."

Stevie Wonder

(Photo: Motown/Talma)

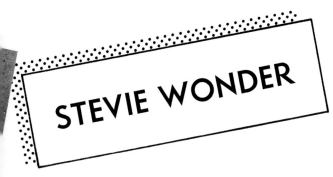

STEVIE WONDER

Unaided, his gait is a purposeful one. He moves with assurance and aplomb, unfettered by a quarter century of blindness. Only the everpresent shades and the slight tilt of his head reveal his affliction. The head tilt is a result of an oversensitive auditory sense. (Wonder hears, almost painfully, sounds that sighted persons take for granted.)

Wonder's world is forever dark, absent of any form, image, or color, but it is certainly not bleak. As with Beethoven, who composed his most vibrant works while completely deaf, Wonder's lack of ocular perception has allowed him an inner vision that few humans have ever experienced. As his one-time mentor Berry Gordy, founder of Motown, has said: "Technically, Stevie is blind. But," he adds with amazement, "he is *not* blind as far as I'm concerned. He sees better than any of us!"

Gordy was first introduced to Wonder in 1961 by Ronnie White of the Miracles. Wonder was a skinny little ten-year-old named Stevland Morris, and Motown Records was little more than a broken-down garage converted into a studio in the thick of Detroit's ghetto. Gordy, working closely with a songwriter named William "Smoky" Robinson, Jr., was just beginning to weave his way into the music industry, compiling an impressive roster of acts including the Four Tops, the Supremes, the Temptations, and Martha and the Vandellas.

Gordy signed Stevland to a contract, changed his moniker to Little Stevie Wonder, and set about molding his young, raw talent into the cool professionalism that was fast becoming the signature of a Motown act.

Two years later Wonder took to the road as a part of the now famous Motown Revue, traveling cross-country with a cavalcade of his fellow performers. The troupe—the aforementioned Tops,

Tempts, Supremes, Miracles, et al.—watched as Wonder, this frail twelve-year-old, came onstage, his harmonica seeming too large for his diminutive frame, and played until, night after night, the audience was on its feet, ecstatic.

A nationwide hit—"Fingertips Part 1 and 2"—followed. Wonder was dubbed the Twelve-year-old Genius. Levi Stubbs, lead vocalist for the Tops, remarked, "With Stevie we always sensed there was something very very special about him. This wasn't just a little kid who could sing or whatever—man, he had *everything!*"

Diana Ross saw him as "someone who was born with a very unique gift. He developed as he grew older, naturally, but as a youngster his grasp of music overwhelmed us all."

With the success of "Fingertips," it became apparent that Wonder would continue his musical career. At an age when most of us strayed no farther from home than the playground, Wonder's songs were topping the charts consistently; he was a star.

By age twenty-one, he had become one of the nation's most prestigious black recording stars. His music had become predictably commercial (a specialty that Motown favored)—good, funky soul yet nothing out of the ordinary. Berry Gordy felt that Wonder would maintain his direction along the smooth road of AM hit after AM hit.

But twenty-one is an unpredictable age, a time when the often-disturbing, constantly challenging process of becoming yourself shifts into high gear, a time when the awful realization of the possibility of controlling your own destiny takes hold. No one felt that newly emerging strength more than Wonder. Now that he was twenty-one, all his earnings, reported to be in the millions, became his to do with as he pleased (they had been conserved by a state-appointed guardian until he became of legal age).

162

Wonder began to question his direction, both musically and personally. "It was time for a change," he reflected, an inflection of pride in his voice. "Spiritually, I had gone as far as I could. Musically, there were new things I wanted to attempt. I asked myself the question of Where was I going? What did I want to do? I had to see and *feel* what I wanted. I had to find out for sure what my destiny was."

With only slight protest from Gordy ("After all," a friend confided, "Berry knew that Stevie was a big moneymaker [for the company]; he was willing to let him try his own thing"), Wonder went into the studio, intent on producing an album that depicted *him*—his thoughts, his lifestyle, his *being;* a body of songs that concentrated on the core of his creativity rather than the commercial potential of that gift. He'd discovered the synthesizer ("It added a whole new dimension to my music"). He felt unburdened, exploding with a thousand new ideas. The first proof of maturation was revealed in *Music of My Mind,* a piece of work that was as much of himself as it was *about* himself.

It sold well over a million copies.

With *Music of My Mind,* Wonder captured a newer, more diverse audience. His perfect blend of keyboard rhythms—some churningly funky, others soothing and gentle—and insightful lyrics drew the attention of the majority of the rock world. Critics and the public alike favored it with exceptional plaudits. "I felt something happening while I was working on it," Wonder explained. "I felt very much in control of the work. I was very satisfied with the end product."

The monetary success of *Music of My Mind* convinced Motown that no matter where Wonder wandered with his music, it would not diminish his selling power. So they let him be. Freed completely from

163

the chains of commerciality, Wonder began to court his new audience. He went on a major tour with the Stones, traveling with his group Wonderlove, receiving excellent notices for his performances. His songwriting became prolific; it was as if he had discovered a well of material deep inside himself and it was bubbling over, begging to be tapped.

Wonder's next album, *Talking Book,* was replete with magic, and the singles "Superstition" and "You Are the Sunshine of My Life" were national hits.

In June 1973 came *Innervisions,* a deeply personal album in which Wonder undertook to further explain his spiritual as well as emotional relationship with his music. The clearly devout nature of the album appeared almost prophetic. Two months later, Wonder lay in a hospital bed, in a coma, the result of a near-fatal automobile accident.

It took months but he did fully recover. However, even after he emerged from the coma, he remained incommunicado to all but his closest friends. When he felt well enough to work again, he began to speak publicly of the visions and dreams he had "been blessed with" while lying in his hospital bed, far within a nether world. "I was shown the true meaning of my life," he marveled. "Through the grace of God, I now realize the purpose of my music."

Wonder set to work furiously, convinced that his newly discovered "innervisions," applied within his music, could somehow effect change in society. He knew he was being listened to seriously by millions. He wanted to convey his private thoughts, what he called his sacred understanding, to his public.

With three Grammys under his belt (for *Innervisions* he was awarded Album of the Year plus Best Pop Vocalist and Best Male R and B Vocalist), Wonder announced he was going into the studio to commence work on his most ambitious project to date. For more than a year and a half, he remained secreted in a studio, spending virtually all his waking hours with the muse.

Rumors about the material he had written abounded; it was said that he was ripping out fantastically advanced tunes at an incredible pace, that he was somehow attempting to cram all his accumulated knowledge into one huge statement—a masterpiece.

In October 1976, Wonder was finished. The album was titled *Songs in the Key of Life* and was, in Wonder's words, "only a conglomerate of thoughts in my subconscious that my Maker decided to give me the strength to bring to fruition. I've never considered myself an orator nor a politician, only a person who is fortunate enough, thanks to all of you, to become an artist given a chance to express the way he feels and hopefully the feelings of many other people. I hope, above all, that this album brings you love."

Songs in the Key of Life was a truly phenomenal work; perhaps one unequaled yet by any other young performer. (Wonder was in his mid-twenties when he wrote most of the material.) The album contained twenty-one songs and garnered Wonder several awards. It was everything the man had promised and more. Even today, more than four years after its release, it stands as a highly accomplished, unique work. It is, as one musician friend was overheard to say, "something we all can look at and use as a gauge for our own talent."

(Wonder's newest LP, *Stevie Wonder's Journey Through the Secret Life of Plants*, is actually the soundtrack from an as yet unfilmed movie. As such, it consists mostly of instrumentals. It is an excellent album; nonetheless, it is too much a soundtrack to be considered Wonder's next major work.)

I last spoke with Stevie at the day-long debut party celebrating the

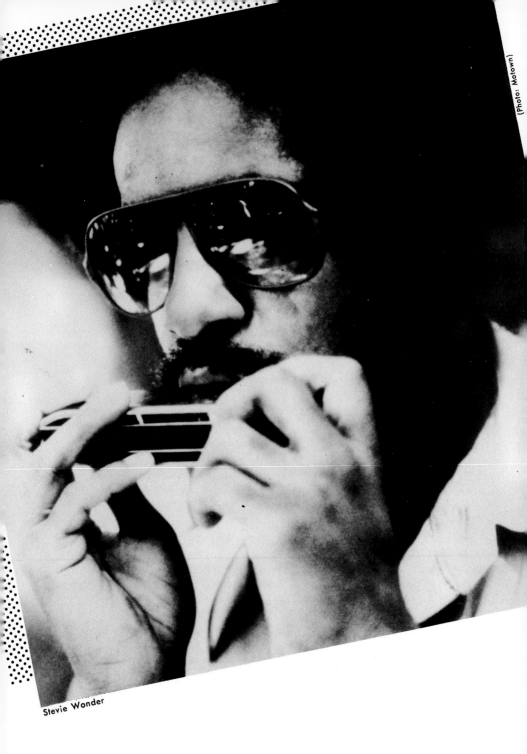

Stevie Wonder

release of *Songs*. It was a huge celebration, held at the famed
Longview Farms, a New England retreat frequented by rock's
higher echelon. Among a hundred acres of farmland, Longview
consists of an impressive and highly regarded fully staffed recording
studio. The festivities were lacking in no manner; the press was
treated to mounds of catered food and an open bar serving
good, strong drinks.

The preliminaries done, the press was escorted into the studio to
hear the album. Wonder was already there, the master tape cradled
in his arms. He was dressed in a tailored whiter-than-white cowboy
suit. Around his waist he wore a thick gunbelt decorated with
facsimile silver bullets. In the holster was a mockup of the album
cover, and the stitching on the gunbelt read: "Number One with a
Bullet"—a reference to the anticipated popularity of the album.
(Of course, in retrospect none of this promotion nonsense was
necessary; the songs spoke for themselves. But strange are the
workings of record-company publicity people.)

Stevie was seated at the studio's wide console. His fingers,
super-sensitive because of his blindness, deftly placed the tape on
the reels of the machine. He sat forward in his chair, eager, maybe
anxious, and spoke: "I want to thank my brother for his help on
this album. I want to thank my collaborators, everyone who has
been with me through the creation of this album. This album is
about love. It's about everything I've learned about love. Now,
please join me in singing of the day when love will reign."

With that Wonder pressed the ON button at the console, smiled
warmly, and let the music begin. An hour into the album, the usually
jaded members of the press were glowing with bliss. Notebooks
had been abandoned, replaced by smiles and impromptu dancing.
It was then, at the height of frivolity, that Wonder leaned toward
his brother, a pure peal of laughter in his throat, and sang out:
"We did it! Thank you, God—we did it!"

John Scher

FEED YOUR BODY

It is virtually impossible to find anyone in this business who dislikes Cy Kocis. Cy, a karate expert who is most comfortable dressed in shorts and a T-shirt, with a bandanna wrapped around a balding head, is an excellent cook. But more than that, he is the premier rock 'n' roll chef.

In a business where "on the road" food has always meant cold cuts, potato salad, and stale rolls, Cy (along with his former boss John Scher) was the first person to introduce hot meals backstage. That was five years ago. Cy, whose original home kitchen was backstage at Passaic, New Jersey's, Capitol Theatre, is frequently hired to provide repast during the tours of many of the nation's top artists.

Cy's philosophy is simple: "It's pretty much third-grade psychology, but it makes sense. Good food and good drink may not necessarily make for a good show but it certainly helps. In '75, John [Scher] asked me to help out with the food preparation at the Capitol. At that time it was mostly catered-type stuff—cold cuts and the like. I told him for the same amount of money I could make a hot meal for the groups.

"John gave me the go ahead, and that's how it started. I knew I was doing something right when not too long afterwards Pink Floyd played the Capitol and told me that the food was the best they'd ever had on the road.

"Well, from there John and I decided to expand the food service until now I have a full kitchen backstage and a traveling kitchen [a two-ton truck outfitted with all the requirements] that I take on the road.

"Of course, as we expanded, so did the artists' requests. In the beginning we served one hot meal, and that was it. Now you have people coming to the theater or concert hall at 9:00 a.m. [the

169

sound men and roadies] and working through the show into the next morning. So I'm usually set up to serve three meals a day plus any special requests the artist may have."

Each band's contract contains a rider specifying what food and beverages are to be provided; however, Cy uses riders only as a guide or outline. He prefers to speak directly to the road manager, working on the premise that the manager, an integral member of the touring ensemble, knows the *exact* preferences of the artists. Whereas the rider may simply indicate "full course dinner," the manager is able to explain to Cy that, for instance, the band must eat *after* the show, because preshow jitters and food don't mix, or that, in the case of many of the English bands, the request for beer means English beer or ale if possible.

"We spend between a thousand and fifteen hundred dollars on each show," Cy explains. "That would include everything—beverages and food. We feed the house crew, the band, and their entourage. I say I'm cooking for anywhere from twenty-five to thirty-five people each show. I'm very particular in my work. I buy everything myself because I don't trust anyone else. I buy the produce, I buy the meat, the fruit, the fish . . . I go to the bakery. It is important to me that the band comes away from a meal that I have prepared both well fed and satisfied. There's really no reason why a band has to suffer foodwise on the road. It may take a little more time, but it's definitely worth it as far as I'm concerned."

As far as the bands are concerned, it is more than worth it. During the Rolling Thunder tour, Dylan and Baez took the time to lead their people in a standing ovation for Cy at the completion of a five-course dinner. Jazz singer Al Jarreau's wife (both Al and his wife are vegetarians) cajoled Cy into revealing his vegetable-entrée recipes for use in their home. The Grateful Dead's Weir and Lesh

both said, "There really isn't anyone else we trust on the road.
Havin' Cy around is a lot like bringin' Mom's kitchen with you."

But the best compliment Cy has received comes in the form of
emulation. Suddenly, more and more bands are hiring professional
chefs to take with them on tour. The business of good eating is
becoming a priority among the rock people. Not that the onslaught
of competition has Cy in the least bit worried. As he remarked:
"KISS were going out on the road for their summer '79 tour.
I heard they hired two women to do all the cooking. One night I'm
working at the Capitol and both of the women showed up. 'We just
wanted to meet you and watch you work,' one of them said.
'Every place we've been, we've heard about you and your cooking.'
And that's the kind of thing that really makes me feel good.
Makes me feel like I'm doing something right, anyway."

FROM CY'S FILES:

The two biggest beers in rock 'n' roll are Budweiser and Heineken.
Have enough of both around, and everybody's happy.

The largest riders belong to the Beach Boys and Yes.

When a crew arrives in the morning, before breakfast, they are
generally in an ugly mood. Feed first, talk later.

In general, those artists more artistically inclined tend to be easier
to deal with.

The newer bands, those who haven't been on the scene that long,
usually will be brash and demanding. Again, a lot of this attitude
disappears after they are fed. Find the road manager, develop
a rapport, and feed.

171

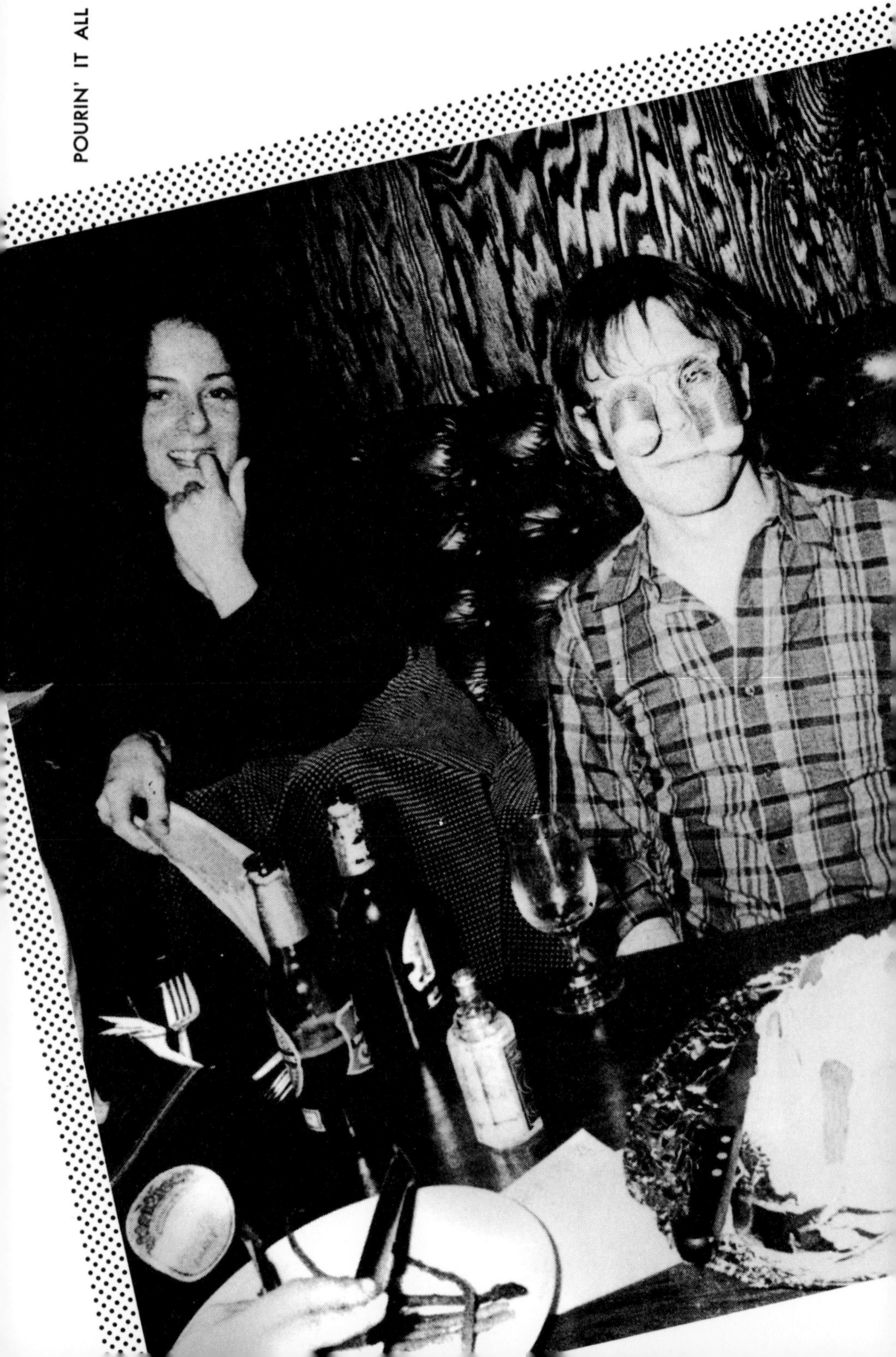

Weir's birthday party.

SOME PREFERENCES:

Bob Dylan: Elaborate rider but not unreasonable. On Rolling Thunder tour, rider included three meals a day. Hot breakfast at 9:00 a.m. Three entrées at dinner. Hors d'oeuvres. Requested a case or so of good imported wine. Feeding seventy people at each sitting. Note: Leave Dylan alone; don't bother him.

Grateful Dead: A number of vegetarians on the crew. The band likes steak, good wine, and Heineken.

Boston: Into fine wines. Specified Château Modet 1970.

Patti Smith: Nothing elaborate. One request—that everyone be fed.

Beach Boys: Management requests a huge amount of food to be prepared and put out on the table. Most of it goes to waste. It appears to be more for show than anything else.

Elvis Costello: Requests English beer and ale in the dressing room.

The Outlaws: Beer and steak.

Marshall Tucker Band: Beer and steak; a couple of bottles of Jack Daniel's on hand.

Van Morrison: Specified in his rider—please, no beer.

Billy Joel: Asked for breakfast, lunch, and dinner. Two bottles each in dressing room of red and white wine and Perrier. Likes Heineken.

Bruce Springsteen: Band likes beer. Nothing else in particular. Two entrées at dinner. "Whatever you want, Cy. It's okay with me."

Jackson Browne: Same as Springsteen. Anything I want to serve.

(Photo: Francesco Scavullo/1980)

Judy Collins

(Photo: Aucoin Management/Press C

KISS

na Ross

(Photo: Motown)

Ronstadt

(Photo: Jim Shea)

Judy Collins: Special request for dressing room—wildflowers and chicken soup.

Eddie Money: Rider is normal one. Gets bottles of Scotch sent backstage by fans.

Linda Ronstadt: Requests California wines.

Diana Ross: Elaborate lunch. In the dressing room—bottle of Perrier, bottle of Courvoisier, Scotch, bourbon, vodka, bottle of French Chablis.

George Benson: Nothing special. Very easy to work with. Likes hors d'oeuvres before dinner.

Cheap Trick: Japanese beer and four packs of playing cards.

KISS: Very civilized. Want lunch and dinner. Request Mouton Cadet wine when available.

The Dead, 1979. Left to right: Hart, Lesh, Donna Godchaux, Garcia, Weir, Kreutzmann. Front: Keith Godchaux. Keith and Donna are no longer with the band

THE GRATEFUL DEAD

We used to play for Silver, but now we play for life
—"Jack Straw"
Hunter/Garcia

If there is one American group that best epitomizes the entire
spectrum of rock 'n' roll, that group is the Grateful Dead. For fifteen
years, the Dead has been turning out albums and putting on
concerts that have won the group great acclaim (and a plethora
of fiercely loyal fans—the notable Deadheads) as well as horrific
criticism. With the Dead, it's a matter of love or hate; either you're
crazy about them or you simply can't stand them. There is no
middle ground.

The Dead's history is long and complicated, but if it were to be
considered in a sort of "Cliff's Notes" manner it would read
something like this: They were primarily responsible (along with their
friends the Jefferson Airplane, Quicksilver Messenger Service,
Janis Joplin, and the Charlatans) for the Haight-Ashbury summer of
'66. They were a driving force behind novelist Ken Kesey's famous
Acid Tests. They were one of the first groups (pre-Woodstock)
to play rock 'n' roll outdoors in front of huge crowds. They performed
at Woodstock, Altamont, and Watkins Glen.

Some of their most ardent fans include Kesey, Timothy Leary,
Richard Alpert (Baba Ram Dass), Yale professor and author
Charles Reich (*The Greening of America*), basketball star Bill Walton,
and the internationally feared and renowned Hell's Angels.

Their success has been accompained by pain and failure. *American
Beauty*, released in 1970, their fifth LP and the one that won them
across-the-board acclaim, was made during a time of great personal
tragedies, including deaths (Lesh's father died of cancer, and
Garcia's mother was killed in an automobile accident). Their 1972
European tour was a huge success; yet it foreshadowed the death
of vocalist Pigpen (Ron McKernan). Shortly after the tour, Pigpen
succumbed to a serious bout with alcohol.

They began their own record company in 1975. Appropriately, the logo was that of a half-laughing, half-cynical-looking crow. At the time it was explained that the crow was chosen so that "if the company fails, we won't have to eat crow. It's already eaten us." The venture failed. They developed their own travel company, Fly-by-Night, to be available for rock 'n' roll touring exclusively, and it, too, failed.

There was the well-known ripoff perpetrated by Mickey Hart's father a number of years ago and a similar one, the details of which have never been released, five years ago.

In the fall of 1978 they traveled to Egypt's Great Pyramid, built a stage at the monument's base, and performed before a rapturous multitude. Garcia, the Dead's lead axman, said of that trip: "We found out that Anwar Sadat and his wife were great fans of ours. It also came to our attention that many Egyptians enjoyed our music. So we set it up with their Office of Culture, invited some of their musicians to join us in a jam, and a good time was had by all."

If one could sum up the Dead's career in a word, that word would have to be perseverance. But it's much more than that. It's talent, intellect, the willingness to take chances, a great deal of love, a great deal of respect for each other, and a half dozen other ideals that make a family work. And that's precisely what the Greatful Dead is: a family.

BOB WEIR

"This is my work, and on any given night it's terrific, and it's absolute hell on a bad night. If I'm having a bad night on stage, you wouldn't want to be in my shoes.

"An artist must take into consideration the parameters in which he is

(Photo: Lookout Studios)

working. You've got to know who you're writing for, who your
audience is. If nobody understands you but the gods and the
muses, then how much good are you doing?

"With the Dead onstage there are those moments of electricity . . .
and the audience is very much a part of those moments—moments
when everybody hears the same thing instantaneously and it
becomes very transcendental. It goes beyond emotion or intellect
at that point. Actually it's a marriage between emotion and intellect.
I liken it to the divine, a moment of real divineness. It's real
inspirational, real palpable inspiration. Yet I also happen to know
that there are kids out there who are either too asleep or too
drowned out or what have you and are not open enough to receive
that feeling. But that's sort of like not being open enough to
receive a bus when it's coming your way! But by and large, the
people in the audience do feel that electricity, that energy.

"We strive for that moment a lot on stage, and sometimes it works
and sometimes it doesn't. But it's a rare night that the band and I
can't deliver a little sunshine. I always felt that if we had *played*
at Altamont (we never *did* get onstage; things got so heavy that
the Stones just wanted to play first and split), we could've changed
the vibes. It's possible. You know, we would have done 'Lovelights'
or something, and maybe the whole thing would have been
different, but it didn't work out that way. That place was like hell.
It looked like . . . well, the sky had a real hellish look, real dark
and eerie just like a Hieronymous Bosch painting, and it *smelled*
like hell. It got cold, and people were burning plastic and stuff to
keep warm. It was just a mess. You could feel the vibes had turned
around . . . it was the wrong time. It kind of showed all the flower
people that the flower generation was bullshit. Everybody tried
to vibe away the badness—one last huge attempt for the flower
generation—but it all came back at them twice as bad. It was a
lesson for *all* of us, and I hope we all learned from it."

"Yet a time did exist when the 'good vibrations' cliché was a reality, did work in a way, didn't it?"

"Yes, for a while. The most amazing thing thus far with the Dead was being involved with the inception of the 'psychedelic era' or what have you. When the Dead became involved with Kesey's Acid Tests—the original ones—that was the most amazing single thing that has ever happened to me. It was one big party, one adventure incarnate. We were living on the edge all the time for a good, sustained period of time. It built to a fever pitch that was incredible. It had an amazing amount of energy. Of course, as soon as the media found out about it, it was over. As soon as it was defined as a 'high scene,' that was it.

"I don't know how to describe exactly what the end felt like or when it came about, but let's just say as soon as people heard about it in Ohio, it was over."

ROBERT HUNTER

". . . It was at the old Fillmore that I got hit real heavy with some LSD by some acid assassins. It was a night when just everything went bonkers. For all I know, it might even have been a tragic trip. It took me two years to piece it together after that one. I was not too happy about that. I just used up too much energy. There was a point where I was lying back, looking up at the sky at a gold bar that was radiating energy—an intense light like the light of the sun—and I suddenly realized that light was my own energy pouring out of me and I didn't have any way of stopping it. There was no dam I could put on it. I just saw a year, two years of energy pouring out of this hole. And it took just about that much time to get all that energy back."

Hunter, the Dead's lyricist, speaks with an intelligence and aplomb that are rare among rock personalities. He is as serious about prose and poetry as he is about his lyrics. He's comfortable expounding on the works of Pound, Blake, or Eliot. His conversation is peppered with memorized verses from the writers he admires.

Hunter met Garcia shortly after both had left the army. Originally they came together as a folk act, "the hottest folk duo in Northern California." As a duo, they appeared at the Monterey Pop Festival on the same bill with Dylan. It was the same year the festival presented such then-unknowns as Hendrix, Joplin, and the Mamas and the Papas.

When Garcia hooked up with the infamous North Beach crowd (forming the Warlocks, an early incarnation of the Dead), he approached Hunter with the idea that Hunter become the lyricist for the group.

Hunter recalls, "At that point I figured why not? Although songwriting hadn't occurred to me, I had already written three novels, a whole bunch of short stories, and reams of poetry. That was the direction I *thought* I was heading in. I had every intention of becoming a *writer*, as opposed to a lyricist. But as it happens, as it was *supposed* happen, Garcia and I realized that our thought processes came together very well in terms of songwriting.

"By mutual agreement, I'll present Jerry with the lyrics I've written and purposely *not* influence him with my melodic structure unless he asks me. Since I do write with a guitar, he may say, 'I'm not quite sure what you had in mind here. This doesn't quite make sense,' and then I'll play him a couple of chords and show him how I conceived of the rhythm and the melody. Garcia will then say, 'Okay, I get it,' and then we start to work on word deletions or sentence changes so that the words fit into the melodic structure he's developing. There are times when he'll take what I give him whole,

185

The Grateful Dead, 1970. Left to right: Kreutzmann, Pigpen, Weir, Hart, and Lesh. Front: "Captain Trips" Garcia.

Backstage at the Capitol Theater. Left to right: Bob Weir, John Scher, and Road Manager Jon McIntyre.

ELVIS, ALONE, IN MEMPHIS

In truth, once he had become *Elvis,* once the curled upper lip that smacked of defiance, the pelvis that refused to remain inert, and the burnt-honey voice became as unmistakable as birthmarks, he would never know what it meant to be alone again. Graceland, for all its opulence, was more a prison than a paradise. Despite the sprawling grounds, the pool, the tennis and racquetball courts, the gymnasium, and the mansion itself, it remained a fortified island and became a private hell.

Every single day, for a decade, dozens of fans waited at the gates in the unlikely event that he would venture forth from the estate into the real world. Every single day. On the rare occasions when he did dare go anywhere, he set out in a caravan of limousines, a half dozen bodyguards in constant attendance. He was one of the most famous persons in the world. There was nowhere he could go to escape from the fact.

A thousand stories are told concerning the day of his death. A famous musician I know swears that his guitar would not stay in tune, as if the instrument had chosen to mourn. The president of a local fan club claims to have watched in horror as all her Elvis memorabilia burst into flames. Another fan swears Elvis appeared to her as an apparition. I have read more than a dozen newspaper accounts of attempted suicides.

The anecdote that follows is recounted exactly as it was told to me. Whether it is fact or fiction, I'm not really sure. I choose to believe the story. It represents Elvis as I like to think he always remained— self-mocking, funny, shy, and a little bit humble.

He'd always come after closing, after the alive din of drinking had faded, leaving in its wake the too-familiar musk of cigarette smoke and stale beer. He'd call first, asking if the place were empty. It always was, except for Steven and myself. We both tend bar, and we do the nightly cleanup together.

He called himself El, and laughed self-consciously when, inadvertently, he'd identify himself as Elvis *Presley*. He slurred the name, as if he were awkward with it.

Most the time he wore blue jeans, tight and well faded. Even later, when his belly ballooned, he wore them, although they hung lower on his hips.

One time he had on a black silk shirt, open to his breastbone. "See this shirt?" he laughed, a bad-boy, cutup chortle. "The colonel never liked it. He thought it looked sinister." He pronounced it *sin*-ister, sneering and chuckling as he said it. I think he liked the idea of disobeying his elders.

He loved the jukebox. Leaning against it, with the neon flashing across his face, soaking in the blaring sounds that had begun and maintained his life, he seemed happy. Contented. Once, by mistake, he played "Jailhouse Rock." Steven and I pretended not to notice, but he just shrugged and, after the song had ended, mumbled, "Kid could sing in the old days, huh?"

One Christmas he sent both of us a gift. Steven got a color TV, a beautiful one. He sent me a silk tour jacket. It had brazen white letters on the back, a half foot high, that read:
ELVIS: WORLD TOUR.

I wore the jacket to work the other day. Some guy asked me if I was a roadie. I told him, "No, a friend."

The guy asked for change for the jukebox. Then he started complaining when he found there wasn't any Elvis on the box. "What the hell," he said. "I thought everybody around here was into Elvis."

I threw him out. I figured he should have known better.

Elvis Presley

At Englishtown. Left to right: Unidentified woman, Weir, Hart, Kreutzmann, and Monarch chief John Scher.

LOOSE LIPS

JOHN SCHER—president, Monarch Entertainment Bureau; manager, Renaissance and the Stanky Brown Group; East Coast representative of the Grateful Dead:

"When I think of rock 'n' roll and the eighties, I think in terms of video. Video seems to be the next direction for most of the groups. Not just feature-length films—the Band, Yes, the Dead, and the Who have already done that—but more of a participation in the art of video. Video discs, kind of like a combination of a record and a miniature movie, should be available within five years. Instead of buying an album, the customer gets a disc which contains not only the group's new songs but also a film of them performing the tunes. He goes home, inserts it into a home unit, and he's got his very own private concert!

"We already have closed-circuit cameras at all of our shows. The audience seems to enjoy watching the bands in concert and onscreen at the same time. Also, with the exception of the first few rows of seats, our cameras make for better viewing for more people than is possible in a normal concert situation, particularly in a larger hall.

"I'm not too sure how well the huge outdoor concerts will fare in the future. Our shows at the Meadowlands [seating one hundred thousand and up] have been abandoned for the time being, and our last big success [the Grateful Dead Englishtown concert, with three hundred thousand in attendance] brought us a lot of flak from the townspeople. For now, I'd have to say that outdoor concerts are a thing of the past.

"I think the heavy-metal sound's just about had it. It seems to me that people are responding more and more to singer-songwriters and their bands. As any promoter will tell you, the big acts right now are Billy Joel, Eddie Money, Costello, Springsteen, and Meat Loaf."

JON LANDAU—former associate editor of *Rolling Stone*, currently president of Jon Landau Management, exclusive representation of Bruce Springsteen:

"I don't necessarily feel as if I've gone over to the enemy's side since I left *Stone* and took up managing, but I have been able to get a different perspective on the matter—I understand now just exactly how a bad review of an album, or a good one, for that matter, can affect an artist. Or how a writer's passing comment in an article can really hurt someone. A person works on an album for two, three years, puts everything he's got into it, and a critic can dismiss the whole project as trash in a matter of a couple of hundred words. Sad but true.

"I suppose I've done that in my time, though certainly not intentionally. I guess I've learned to take myself less seriously when it comes to writing about rock. And I've come to realize exactly what goes into a record, into the production of a record—the work that goes into taking a song that was written on an acoustic guitar or a piano, say, and following it along until the band learns it, the artist works it out, and it's all finally perfected and put on vinyl. I hope I'll be able to bring all that knowledge with me each time I write a piece.

"In terms of music, the last few years and those upcoming seem a lot like the late sixties to me. There are some real good songwriters and some real good bands around. The English bands—Costello and the Attractions, Parker and the Rumor, Nick Lowe, Dave Edmunds—are very strong right now. And there seems to be a trend back to writing short, three-minute pieces, the kind of stuff that the Beatles and the Stones used to write so well. Bruce's next album, after a live one, will be full of short pieces—all of them, in my very biased opinion, great."

196

BILL GRAHAM—promoter, founder of legendary Fillmore East and Fillmore West concert halls, head of Wolfgang Productions:

"I've given up trying to figure out where this business is heading. Each time I think I've left it for good, something comes up and I find myself right back where I started. I don't think you'll ever see the Fillmores open again—somebody tried that with the Fillmore East a couple of years back, but from what I understand, they lost a great deal of money in a very short time.

"I enjoy being on the production and managing end of things these days. I learned quite a bit about this business, and I try to apply what I've learned to my production work. Eddie Money was Wolfgang Productions' first acquisition, and he's done right by us. We'll be trying to pick up a few more artists in the future.

"Actually, when I'm confronted with the 1980s I can't help but think about how old we're all getting to be. When I started in this business I never figured I'd be able to remain in it after thirty years old. Now most the rock stars I know are staring forty in the face!"

ALLEN FREY: A.R.S.E. Management, personal management for Elvis Costello and Graham Parker:

"The future of rock 'n' roll? I don't think it will be much different than it has in the last few years. As Costello said, 'America may have invented rock 'n' roll, but the English *play* rock 'n' roll.' I suppose we'll continue to make the American rockers squirm."

MIKE APPEL—Laurel Canyon Productions; credited with discovering Bruce Springsteen:

"When Springsteen first came into my office, I knew right then that this was a talent to be reckoned with. I didn't tell Springsteen that—I sent him home and told him to practice for a while and come back in a couple of days. Well, he went to California to visit his parents, and when he came back the stuff he showed me was twice as good as before. I called John Hammond at Columbia and brought Bruce up there to see him. As they say, the rest is history.

"Contrary to popular belief, I still think Bruce is a tremendously talented songwriter, maybe the best going right now. I also think he was responsible for the current outpouring of songwriters—I can't imagine Costello or Parker or Meat Loaf being as popular as they are if Bruce hadn't paved the way.

"I suppose what I'd most like to see happen is another Springsteen walk through the doors of Laurel Canyon. I'd like to do the same for him that I did for Bruce."

GOLD RECORD Awarded by the RIAA (Recording Industry of America Association), the designation refers to an album that has sold five hundred thousand copies or a single (45rpm) that has sold one million copies. See Platinum record.

MAGAZINES, THE In rock 'n' roll parlance, when we refer to "the magazines," we usually mean *Rolling Stone, NME* (New Musical Express), *Circus, Creem, Trouser Press, Punk, High Times, Phonograph, New York Rocker,* and *Melody Maker. See also* Trade magazines.

MULTITRACK RECORDING Tape recording using several tracks upon which music can be recorded. On a twenty-four-track recording, twenty-four different instruments or voices can be separately recorded (although in practice, of course, more than one track is recorded at a time). Many of the tracks are often used to double or triple a guitar lead or to strengthen a weak vocal. When different tracks are recorded at different times, you can sing "harmony" with yourself or play two or three or more instruments on one recording. Twenty-four-track recording is the most often used for rock, but eight-, sixteen-, and thirty-two-track formats are also used at times.

PLATINUM RECORD An album that has sold one million copies or a single (45rpm) that has sold two million copies. *See also* Gold record.

PRODUCER The person who produces an artist—taking responsibility for the artist's progress, from signing of the contract through to completion of the record.

PROMOTER A person who runs a concert hall and promotes concerts throughout her or his area, whether at the promoter's hall or at a stadium, rented facility, or college. On the East Coast

John Scher and Ron Delsener are the top promoters. On the West Coast Bill Graham is still considered father of the clan.

RECORDING STUDIOS Some of the best are Record Plant East and Record Plant West, MediaSound, Studio 55, Trident, Caribou, Sigma Sound Studios, Eras Recording Studios, and Alpha.

RIAA Recording Industry of America Association. The RIAA serves the record industry in much the same way in which the AMA serves the medical industry. As the official organ of the industry, the RIAA monitors all record sales and presents gold- and platinum-record certificates when warranted.

ROADIES The road crew, responsible for setting up and breaking down all the equipment used by a performer or group. Roadies are usually hired for the duration of a tour and paid a salary.

SECURITY The security guards at a concert whose main function is to keep order while the concert is in progress and to maintain a good distance between the fans and the performers. Most promoters have their own staffs of guards.

TIPSHEETS Kal Rudman's Friday Morning Quarterback and Bill Hard's FMQB Album Report. The Bibles of radio stations' program directors. Tipsheets are used much like their racing-world counterparts—the director relies on the trained "ear" of the tipster to second guess the record-buying public, predicting what songs they will choose as their favorites, thereby guaranteeing that the director's upcoming playlist reflects the public's current musical tastes.

TRADE MAGAZINES Also called simply "the trades," Billboard, Cashbox, and Record World report weekly on all the activity within the industry. They compile charts each week, indicating how much airplay records have received that week. The charts show the popularity of a record, which is usually followed by increased sales. See also Magazines, the.

204

DIGITAL DELAY LINE (DDL) An advanced electronic device that intercepts a note of music, as it is being fed into a tape machine ("reading" the note as an electronic signal), transposes the note up or down a harmonic third, and inserts it into the tape machine along with the original note, producing harmony. Using this device, a singer can sing in harmony with himself or herself. The DDL can be used to produce guitar harmony in the same manner.

DIGITAL RECORDING The newest advance in recording technology. In its simplest form, digital recording marks the introduction of computers into the recording process. As the artist records on tape, the sound is translated into a systems code and programmed into a computer. Thus, the problems inherent in using tape—residual noise, accidents, etc.—are eliminated. The electronic code of digital recording cannot fluctuate, regardless of environmental conditions. Therefore, a higher standard of excellence is possible with digital.

DOLBY DDX An electronic noise suppressor. The DDX filters out high-end noise, enabling the engineer to produce a much cleaner master tape.

ENGINEER The person who oversees the recording equipment in a studio and supervises its operation, in addition to operating some of the equipment. A good engineer can make the difference between a decent record and a great one. Some of the best at this time are Jim Iovine, Todd Rundgren, Peter Klesey, Phil Ramone, Bob Clearmountain, and Bob Matthews.

FANZINE A magazine, often mimeographed or offset, devoted to a single artist or group and published solely for the devoted fan. Examples are *Thunder Road* (the Bruce Springsteen fanzine) and *Relix* (the Grateful Dead fanzine).

TRADE TALK: A GLOSSARY

A AND R PERSON An Artist and Repertoire representative. At one time an A and R person was responsible for seeking out songs for a group to perform. Over the years, as more and more artists have been writing their own material, the A and R person's job has evolved into talent acquisition and hooking up performers with producers.

APHEX AURAL EXCITER An electronic device that makes possible a studio effect enhancing the sound in a recording. The Aphex must be leased from its inventor—it cannot be purchased. If it is used, credit must be given on the album.

ARBITRON RATING SYSTEM A system that rates the percentage of the listening audience tuned in to each radio station at a given time. Arbitron's ratings are determined by telephone survey. The ratings are held in high regard—they can directly affect the amount of advertising a station sells.

ASCAP The American Society of Composers, Authors, and Publishers. ASCAP's function (for our purposes) is to determine how often a recording is played on radio or television and then to calculate and collect the royalties due the composer or composers. ASCAP also collects royalties for a composer any time her or his composition is performed for profit. For example, if a singer chooses a particular song for his or her concert repertoire, the composer receives a royalty payment each time the artist performs the song.

BULLET, WITH A Industry slang referring to a record that is steadily moving up the charts. A bullet is actually a typographical symbol placed beside the title of the record to indicate its increased popularity.